EDUCATION
FOR
ANNIHILATION

To Peter Bergel

Ann Bail Boyer

EDUCATION FOR ANNIHILATION

William H. Boyer

HOGARTH PRESS-HAWAII
Box 6012
Honolulu, Hawaii 96818

LCN 72-88420
SBN 911776-18-4

Printed in the United States of America

He thought he gave
        His country
That last full measure
Of devotion.
Years later
Historians
Who survived
Said the war was
Unnecessary.
                    WHB

ACKNOWLEDGEMENTS:

I wish to acknowledge the helpful comments and criticism I have received from the following people: Herb Alf, the late F. Glenn Austin, Theodore Becker, Catherine Campbell, Joseph D'Enbeau, Larry Jones, Ann Keppel, Victor Kobayashi, and Paul Walsh. And my wife Ann has provided indispensible assistance.

For typing assistance I wish to express my appreciation to Irene Oka and Lana Iwamoto.

WHB

INTRODUCTION

No modern society likes to be considered war-oriented. Yet America, with over half of her national budget allocated to war related expenditures, can hardly escape the label. While many other nations are also war-oriented, the consequences of America's posture are far more serious because it is the most heavily armed nation of all time.

This book is an analysis and critique of the way in which most Americans are educated, formally and informally, to consider war as a necessity in dealing with human problems. Such war education is received through schools, government, churches, businesses, the mass media, and of course the military establishments. In fact, it pervades our entire thought pattern and value system.

America's participation in World War II marked a turning point in our national mentality toward an emphasis upon technology and a de-emphasis upon human worth. While we had entered the war to fight the end-justifies-the-means system of fascism, we soon found our leaders abandoning the policy of hitting only military targets. Even before the tragedies of Hiroshima and Nagasaki, we had joined our allies in raining mass destruction on defenseless civilians in the manner of an enemy whom we considered depraved.

The result was a decline in America's moral sensitivity, to the point where no horror, including the atomic incineration of cities, became too extreme. Means and ends could not be separated, so what had previously been barbarous became a new norm of appropriate conduct.

The war ended, but the weakened moral posture remained. The military values which had supposedly been the characteristics which made the defeated enemy so despicable had now become infused in the American way of life. The values of the conquered and the conqueror were alarmingly similar.

The cold war policy of seeking to contain the spread of Communism gave further impetus to our growing militarism and inadvertently aided Communism through the weakening of our own democratic ideals. Our reliance on violence has led to a massive death toll of both civilian and military personnel in Vietnam and has provided the basic approach to dealing with domestic issues as well. To many of the oppressed peoples of our own land the recent cry for law and order has been viewed as a justification for violence against dissenters.

This increasingly militarized outlook has developed during the very period when atomic war makes military solutions to human conflict intolerably dangerous. Senator Fulbright has pointed out that we live in a time when "the stakes are high indeed: they include not only America's continued greatness but nothing less than the survival of the human race in an era when, for the first time in human history, a living generation has the power of veto over the survival of the next." [1]

Yet most American education continues to be based on old habits of a pre-atomic world that do not recognize the requirements of survival in an atomic age. Most American institutions are not only obsolete, they are part of the problem rather than the solution. They give people a false sense of security, a feeling that experts somewhere are taking care of things. Our society has grown like Topsy with little planning and few self-conscious goals, and now the Damocles sword of World War III threatens not only the life of the nation, but of the entire planet.

While patchwork panaceas have been legislated in abundance, inertia in the American body politic has led to a sterile paucity of imagination. Our political Aladdins have continued to rub their lamps and call upon the faithful genie, technology, only to find that the genie has become an uncontrolled monster. The puerile belief that technology will somehow solve all our problems has been responsible for our rather blind reliance upon new weaponry to bring peace to the world.

Armament programs designed for our national defense may yet be the unwitting handmaiden of national annihilation, for they are based on outdated modes of thought from a substantially different past. Yet most of our leaders who are charged with the task of understanding our problems and developing solutions continue to look at both through a pre-atomic frame of reference.

To the extent that our institutions are based on outdated beliefs, they provide education for annihilation. Contentment with pre-atomic solutions dulls our sensibilities while we plunge headlong toward the brink of disaster. If we are to survive, we must become more aware of the ways in which miseducation occurs. Only then will necessary cultural and institutional change be undertaken.

As man gains more insight into the nature of today's human predicament, and as he increases his knowledge of possible non-military solutions, he will begin to change his environment, his institutions, and even his values — so compelling is the drive for survival. Freed from a myopic reliance upon weaponry and armed with his new social and psychological knowledge, he can begin to reconstruct his culture and his outlook. Education can thus become a future oriented instrument instead of a mere conserver of the past.

Survival will also require that we use technology to serve our most basic values rather than allow it to enslave us in pursuit or peripheral values. The misapplication of technology has now led to the pollution of our air, our water, our food, and our land. The race for more refined weapons technology now portends a level of violence and destruction which far exceeds what sane people can tolerate.

This study tries to contribute to the rational control of international violence by revealing some of the ways in which Americans are taught to support the values and the metaphysics of pre-atomic militarism. It is not assumed that only Americans are being miseducated, but it is assumed that leadership for international reform must begin at home.

It is much more than the military-industrial-political-educational-religious-mass media complex that has locked the mainstream of American life into a dangerously obsolete course of action. The military outlook pervades every dimension of our American system.

New forces for change can be seen, however, especially among the young. Armed with updated social knowledge some of the new generation, and even a few of the old, have escaped the cultural lock-in. New futures are being envisioned, the past is being re-examined, and new strategies for change are being planned and tested.

There are four basic ways in which our survival is threatened and this book focuses on one of them. Over-population, destruction of natural resources, pollution of the biosystem, and international violence are all basic threats to human survival, but section one and two focus only on international violence and the military systems which make war possible. The war system is described as a cultural system in which people have been taught to embrace a way of life that supports military threat systems, so they find it hard to understand what they are doing and even harder to extricate themselves.

The proposed education for survival, which is explained in section three, shows how war systems are related to other systems of planning. A proposal is offered to transform our society, where technology is out of control, by means of a fundamentally different form of planning, which is designed to give men responsible control over technology, especially the technology of war.

CONTENTS

PART III
RECONSTRUCTING AMERICAN SOCIETY
Chapter 6

PART I

TEACHING FOR WAR THROUGH
MILITARY INSTITUTIONS

CHAPTER I

CONDITIONING MILITARY BEHAVIOR

One of the ironies of history is that societies develop institutions to serve people and soon find people serving the institutions. Religiousness has produced organized churches, curiosity has produced schools, and insecurity has produced military establishments. Yet, churches may have little connection with religiousness, schools may have little concern with stimulating curiosity, and military establishments may not contribute to national security. The institutions may even work counter to the original objective.

It is sometimes hard for those within an institution to understand how the institution guides perception and rationalizes its existence. An outside observer may better perceive how the institution shapes the thinking of its members. Social-psychology has shown that normal, honest, sincere men of good will may develop behavior patterns that are primarily reflections of the institutions in which they find themselves.

An institution may continue from generation to generation as a self-perpetuating system. Men who live and work in such an establishment may produce minor changes, but they are likely to be largely guided by the organization, since it is the sub-society of their life. They will tend to develop a vested interest in the institution as it is, and change will be looked upon as a threat. It seems more practical to adapt to the status quo than to promote change. It seems safer to make the most of life within the circumstances in which they find themselves. Often no other alternatives are visible.

Maintaining a governmental or industrial bureaucracy often supersedes the larger purposes of the organization. Systems evolve rituals and procedures which become ends in themselves, and people develop outlooks appropriate to the system.

Many people are able to find satisfaction in a military system. They are often encouraged by the ostensible goals of the system, goals which seem to contain so much that is noble. They may believe they are fighting for their country for greater causes such as ''freedom,'' or to protect their homeland from invasion. It is not surprising that young men who become heroes as defenders of the flag are scarcely motivated to examine the assumptions upon which their ''duty'' is based. In a world in which people seldom serve anyone except themselves, military service suggests a basis for dignity, a chance to serve the common good. The first American patriots fought successfully against imperialism, and their courage and perseverance have become symbols even for the modern soldier. Joining with others in a common cause reduces the sense of isolation and encourages a feeling of importance. Though soldiers often complain about particular aspects of military life, they usually believe that the military forces are vital to the public good.

Modern institutions are so complex that the appearance of institutional value may be an illusion. One's perspective is usually too restricted to enable a very reliable assessment of an entire institution. The interrelationships between one institution and another involve even more complexity. The person who tries to understand, but who waits until all the facts are in before he is willing to decide, will wait forever.

Social behavior can generate an infinite amount of factual information. One way to understand social behavior is to see it through different points of view. Most people in "free" America need more information presented from a variety of viewpoints to keep them from blindly following institutions over which they usually have little or no control.

Ordinarily, people have "freedom" to do only what their culture or institutional subculture has prescribed. A child growing up as a Hopi Indian in northern Arizona will probably be socially cooperative and religiously pantheistic. A child growing up in a middle-class family in New York will probably be competitive and will view nature as an object of control. To the extent that one's life is confined to his own subculture, he will tend to espouse the "party line" of that group.

People tend to think they have made up their own minds when their minds have actually been made up largely by their environment and the comparatively narrow range of experiences they have had. They then tend to universalize their points of view and self-righteously impose them on others.

Man can control his institutions only when he can understand them through a broader perspective. In a democracy, man must be able to be critical of the very institution in which he is involved. He must have a voice in the direction of change rather than simply be caught up in its current. Not only is his freedom at stake, but with the lethal power of modern technology his very existence is also at stake. Therefore, modern man must devise new ways to control institutions, especially those which have destructive power. While new technology and expanding populations create accelerating rates of change, fixation with the habits and structures of the past will continue to cause men to pose the wrong questions and offer the wrong solutions.

Nowhere is this fixation more dangerous than in American military institutions. A fresh look at military habits and structures would be helpful both to military personnel who are too close to the trees to see the forest and to the larger public which, according to our Constitution, must maintain control of military institutions rather than be controlled by them.

I

THE MECHANISMS OF ADJUSTMENT

A. THE LANGUAGE OF ALIENATION AND VILIFICATION

The language of the American soldier reveals some of his novel and even witty modes of adjustment to military environment. Most of his slang, however, represents either bitter commentary on his subordinate role or his attempts to appear tough and virile. One sociologist, analyzing military language, points out that even the common term "GI" is a cynical way in which the soldier has been willing to label himself as Government Issue, similar to a "standardized Army article like a pair of socks, a cake of soap, or a vehicle."[2]

When one's identity is threatened by a hierarchy which is designed to treat him as an object rather than a person, a variety of responses may emerge. A humorous, cynical, frank response provides the soldier with a kind of uneasy adjustment. In those numerous situations when the soldier is powerless to pursue his own interests or to have meaningful human relationships because of the power hierarchy, his language reveals his true feelings. The term "TS," for "tough shit," is used to indicate futile resignation. Cynical contempt for the entire system is implied in the World War II term "SNAFU," which meant, "Situation Normal All Fucked Up," transformed to "fouled" in conventional civilian usage.

This language of alienation is particularly entrenched in the enlisted man's subculture, but the language of toughness and virility is commonplace at all military levels. Its use is so continuous and obsessive that it often appears to serve as compensatory symbolism to prove a "masculinity" that is very much in doubt. Military slang suggests female hatred and an apparent need to prove virility continuously through sexual vilification. As every soldier knows, a dozen or so four-letter words and phrases become descriptive of virtually everything. For that which is most disagreeable, the four-letter words of sexual vilification are endlessly used. While this behavior is not exclusive to the armed forces, the military subculture **intensifies** the more childish modes of adjustment and "brings out primitive aspects of personality."[3] It would appear that training in what the military calls toughness encourages soldiers to "exaggerate and distort the dominant, aggressive quality that is a natural sign of virility. In reaction to the "sissy" qualities which they seek to eradicate or conceal in themselves, they reject everything associated with femininity, especially the values which create disinterested activities and those which lend considerateness and grace to social intercourse."[4]

It is ironic that the military is believed by many people to "build men." If the informal use of language is indicative of the kind of man that is built, he is one who degrades sex, exploits women, and is obsessed with elimination processes, hardly a symbol of the culmination of civilized man.

Sex vilification may be useful for adjustment to military life. The capacity for tenderness and love may be so fundamentally in conflict with the military commitment to violence and killing that sex and its association with love can only be rejected and vilified if institutional adjustment is to be satisfactory. Whereas love involves the affirmation of life, military goals require the well-adjusted soldier to occasionally treat human life lightly or suffer moral conflict. Even more, he must be eager to kill when he is so ordered, and the language of such an institution would be expected to reveal the values it places on human life.

B. RATIONALIZATIONS FOR KILLING

American culture includes a variety of values. In some situations competition, acquisition, indifference, or even brutality may be lauded. In others, the values of individual worth and universal brotherhood may be extolled. The values of the military include many of those found in the larger society, but they minimize a universal humanitarian morality. It makes no sense to have a military establishment unless men are ready to fight. But ''fight'' is often only a euphemism for ''kill.''

The military holds no exclusive claim to teaching violence. American civilians are also taught to be violent and have the dubious distinction of producing one of the world's highest homicide rates. The military, however, is the **only publicly supported** program to institutionalize hatred and promote enemy-psychology. A **national** military system **cannot** promulgate a humane ethic which emphasizes the ''worth of the individual.'' It can encourage humane identification with **American** individuals and "**free world**" individuals, but not with all individuals, for this would psychologically nullify the military mission: It would undercut the task of killing those who become designated as an ''enemy.''

Americans reared on a humane ethic are caught in a moral conflict in the military, resulting in serious problems during compulsory conscription, problems typically ignored by those who have minimal commitment to a humane ethic. There have been cases where military action was literally national defense, where the problem was not whether there is to be killing but whether to kill or be killed. When foreign aggression has such a clear character, a humane ethic is clouded. The Poles, especially those in Warsaw, were clearly faced with this kind of situation. But Americans fighting in Santo Domingo, Vietnam, Laos and Cambodia have not been in an analogous role. These situations are not examples of clear cut national defense against an aggressive enemy. To be sure, Americans are forced into combat in Vietnam where kill-or-be-killed conditions are brought into existence, but the American government has the **choice** of whether to create such a situation.

While an American involved in the military may not be forced to kill for national ''defense,'' he can be certain that if he is forced to kill that American officials will claim that American ''interests'' justify his use of military force. But since some recruits have been taught that all human life is important, an elaborate system of re-education and rationalization for killing must be developed by the military in an attempt to nullify humane morality.

To be sure, many Americans seem to experience no moral conflict in the military because they have not really learned a humane ethic. Some merely learn to increase their moral apathy and insensitivity. The latent psychopaths are encouraged through such materials as a recruiting pamphlet which asks, "How do you stack up as an ACTION GUY?" There is a "self test" where the young man is supposed to answer "Will I really enjoy the chance of adventure in far-away places?" The adjacent picture shows a soldier ready to bring down his rifle butt on the head of another soldier, presumably revealing the real meaning of "action" and "adventure." On another page of the same pamphlet a soldier with an aggressive-psychopathic grimace is stalking with his rifle held ready, and the picture is captioned with the statement, "There's a man-sized job ahead." The pamphlet is titled "The Mark of Man."[5] The theme implies that eagerness to kill is such a "mark."

There is little evidence to reliably document the response of most Americans to the roll of legalized murder which the military may require of them. From Army interviews there is an estimate that at least one-fourth of the men would not kill a designated "enemy,"[6] even though military training aims at teaching soldiers to want to "destroy the enemy" and to develop "aggressiveness."[7] The psychological pressures to kill become much more extreme during actual combat than during training. Moral compunctions become difficult when one's friends are injured, killed, or tortured. Atrocities by both sides have been continually reported in Vietnam as this vicious circle accelerates.

Deep feelings of guilt sometimes develop, as with a mental patient whose psychosis began in the Korean War. He "had raped a woman after killing a Korean man to avenge a dead companion and then had watched the woman kill her child and slit her own throat." He now has a "recurrent nightmare about a Korean woman and her child, drowning in a pool of blood."[8]

In Vietnam, a young Marine said "he felt really sick to his stomach after he had killed a mother and her baby by submachine gun fire. The Marine had killed her husband, presumably a Cong, and she picked up a machine gun and fired and was immediately killed with her child."[9]

An American Air Force officer has said of the bombings of villages "when we are in a bind we unload on the whole area to save the situation. We usually kill more women and kids than we do Viet Cong, but the government troops just aren't available to clean out the villages so this is the only answer."[10]

The same rules in the Vietnam war reward the American military for producing a favorable kill ratio of Viet Cong to American troops.

6

Assessment of the kill ratio is made after the battle through "head counts," and since Viet Cong are Vietnamese, they are not distinguishable from civilians when they are dead. So the military reports everyone who is dead either as "Cong" or as "suspected Cong." Dead civilians become useful to the military by increasing head count ratio, and the dead never contest the classification assigned to them.

The word "enemy" is a remarkably useful psychological device. It serves as a vehicle for bringing together a number of impressions, each of which makes barbarism, violence, and killing easier. It lumps together members of the opposition so that those you kill are believed to lack those human qualities which you connect with your own group. An "enemy" lacks human individuality, possesses evil, is fundamentally dangerous, and is not subject to reform. Its members are at a lower level of life and can be expected to operate through violence, subversion, and hatred. They must, therefore, be feared and dealt with only by counter force. There is no reason to feel sorrow about an enemy being killed; in fact, there is reason to rejoice. As the manual says, soldiers should be taught to "destroy the enemy."

Once the "enemy" psychology is established, a variety of groups can be classified as the enemy. In World War II it was the Fascists. Now it is the Communists. However, in World War II neither Franco nor Batista was usually associated with the word "Fascism," for they were on our side. Nor did we associate the Hungarian "freedom fighters" with Communism, for they were anti-Russian and we had connected Communism with Russia. Yet both Communists and anti-Communists were among the freedom fighters supporting Imre Nagy, a Hungarian nationalist who was also a Communist. Apparently, because so many Americans have turned the world into a black and white choice between "we" and "they," the "freedom fighters" have come to be popularly categorized as anti-Communist, therefore, pro-American.[11]

The same confusion occurred for some time with Tito. And Khruschev's "We will bury you" statement has often been distorted to represent a *military* threat by Russia, though the statement referred to *political* change and was a figurative rather than a literal statement. Khruschev spoke within the frame of reference of Communist dialectical materialism, a deterministic theory of history. He stated, "History is on our side. We will bury you." American selective perception, based on a military metaphysic, transformed the meaning to a literal threat of violence by the Soviet Union.[12]

Words such as "enemy," "free-world," "slave-world," "Fascist," "Communist," and "Cong" serve not merely as classifying devices but as prejudice producing devices. The use of such terms typically provides simplification at the price of reality distortion and lends itself easily to demagoguery and mass media headlines.

Classifying ideas may be a necessary process for intelligent action, but the notion that ideas always correspond with reality assumes too much The manner in which the military imposes words and ideas on the world in fact creates new meanings. When the military translates abstract ideas into concrete forms (e.g. Free world = Taiwan, S. Korea, S. Vietnam, etc.), the public often assumes that the meaning of the word describes the real world. Soon people believe that the meanings perceived are entirely objective.

Classifying an unknown entity as "the enemy" or "the Communists" or "a Communist" often carries the assumption of certain *discovery* of what the *reality* is. In fact, it tends to relieve people of their obligation for further inquiry. This prejudice-producing process is common to modern life, even though it is actually a primitive type of word magic. In civilian life prejudice provides psychological justification for attitudes such as racial discrimination; in military life it similarly provides justification for killing.

C. DIVINE SANCTION

Military pamphlets issued by the chiefs of staff and the Department of Defense often espouse a conception of Americanism which appears to have theological sanction. The ideology of traditional individualism, the official Americanism ideology of the Armed Forces,[13] is based on an early American conception of natural rights and divine authority which is claimed to underlie American political views.[14]

Admiral Radford is quoted in the U.S. Fighting Man's Code as saying that "the American way of life . . . is the closest thing to that which God would have us follow."[15] The part of the "code" which includes the statement that "I will trust in my God and in the United States of America"[16] depicts a symbolic hand of "God" holding the American flag. The Declaration of Independence is cited, that "they are endowed by their Creator with certain unalienable rights," and the statement is treated in a manner which assumes it to be absolute truth rather than culture or ideology. This incomplete view of a theistically grounded America is characteristic of virtually all military pamphlets which are intended to provide thought "guidance" to members of the Armed Forces.

Not only are military materials used to proselytize for theistic belief, but officers provide similar "educational leadership" for interpreting these materials whether or not they have studied theology, history, philosophy, or ethics. And they typically assume that they are entirely justified in their role as military officer to make theological pronouncements. Best known of the extreme evangelist-officers is General Edwin Walker, who in 1960 in Germany used his office to indoctrinate troops to believe in his theological-political beliefs. They were a mixture of Christian fundamentalism and far-right politics that were carried to the point where even the Army found it unacceptable, and General Walker was given a reprimand and a lesser duty. However, after the General announced that most of the top officials of the

American government were either Communists or fellow travelers, even the Department of Defense considered taking legal action against the General's activities in using his military position to influence an election. Under such pressure, he resigned, and as a civilian has since been continuing to promote theological-political fundamentalism of the far right. [17]

In a less extreme manner many other military commanders continue to proselytize. Some are rather surreptitious. Others are like ex Lt. General V. H. Krulak, the Commanding General of the Marine Corps of the Pacific in the mid-1960's, who proudly proclaimed that "Marines who work for me are encouraged to believe in the all encompassing power of a Supreme Being." [18] He did not seem to see any violation of civil liberties in having a government agency proselytize for theological belief, nor did he seem to consider such behavior as a military commander to be a misuse of his special power and authority. His public mandate is merely to teach Marines how to fight. But one of the problems resulting from the view that militarism is grounded in absolute values is that the totalitarian control of military camps provides opportunity not merely for military training but also for physical and psychological coercion. It is, however, a mockery of the idea of religious freedom and of the first Amendment of the Constitution for a Marine commandant in his role as a member of the Armed Forces to encourage Marine subordinates to accept his theological views. How free would one of his junior officers feel, or particularly one of his enlisted men, to proclaim his non-belief openly? With remarkable logic the General said that though Marines "who work for me are encouraged to believe in the all encompassing power of a Supreme Being . . . they are not taught that they are expected to have such a belief." There is not only a problem in logic here, but an apparent failure to understand human social-psychology in an autocratic structure.[19] The fine distinction between being "expected to have such a belief" and being "encouraged to believe" is lost on the average Marine.

It is the American military chaplain, dressed in the garb of a specialist in violence and displaying a cross on his lapel, who represents the most obvious anomaly of the American military establishment. He not only violates the principle of separation of church and state, but also lends the symbolism of religion to provide "moral and spiritual" support to military activity — giving state-supported killing the appearance of divine sanction.

The particular divinity represented by the Armed Forces is a White Anglo-Saxon Protestant version of the Judeo-Christian God. None of the other world religions is represented, even though many members of the Armed Forces are members of other religions. If the *Armed Forces Hymnal* [20] is indicative, there is a military hierarchy of importance among Judaism, Catholicism, and Protestantism. The Hymnal devotes 41 pages to a "Jewish Section," 67 pages to a "Catholic Section," and a whopping 393 pages to a "Protestant Section." The Protestant section offers some especially appropriate hymns such as "A Mighty Fortress Is Our God," and "Onward Christian Soldiers."

Ordinarily members of the Armed Forces have a choice of whether they wish to attend chapel,[21] but in the federal military academies attendance is *compulsory*.[22] This is one of the regulations that appears to defy the first Amendment of the Constitution, which states "Congress shall make no law respecting an establishment of religion." In fact, the entire Chaplain's Corps is probably unconstitutional, but it has never been subjected to a constitutional test.

The chaplains are not merely proselytizers for their own churches, but they are also apologists for military values. In their publications they defend military regimentation as "training for good citizenship"[23] and console parents that their sons and daughters are in an uplifting environment rather than a degrading one. Like a journal of Madison Avenue pitch-men, their official publication says: "See the problem big." This turns out to be religion salesmanship telling the reader (at public expense) that "through Faith and Divine guidance ... religious leaders [serve] youths of the nation as they are assuming their sacred tasks in preserving freedom for all peoples." Religious leaders must also "indoctrinate our youth" and "build into the public mind the firm concept that our men and women in military service are there as maintainers of peace in the world." "Theirs is a service to God and country."[24]

The chaplains, in their special publications, claim to promote "character building, reduce VD rates," provide "personal, religious, and marriage counseling," and make a contribution to "national defense."[25] In *Builders of Faith* they claim that "men and women in the Armed Services will feel the support of the coordinated thinking of all religious forces in America and realize as never before that theirs is a service to God as well as to country."[26] To assume that the U.S. military system coordinates the "thinking of all religious forces in America" is a delusion of grandeur and overlooks some of the most significant religious forces today, many of which are openly anti-military.

Alan Tyler, a veteran of the Korean War, has kept a careful record of the "helpful" contribution he received from the Chaplain's Corps. Though it may not be typical of the every day work of each chaplain, it does give realistic insight into some of the chaplain's services that may not be communicated through official sources.

"The evening of April 12, 1950, at Fort Leonard Wood, Missouri, saw a confused band of freshly-scalped recruits marching into the post chapel. It was our first day at boot camp and this was part of the orientation program. The chapel was a dimly lit, awkwardly built sort of structure which aptly matched our mood and appearance, as we were attired in our newly issued drab O.D. uniforms which were several sizes too large. It had been a day of perpetual humiliations heaped upon us from all quarters, from the shearing and uniforming processes in which we were made to look alike; to the "HERE!", "Yes, Sir!", "No, Sir!" instructions in which we were made to talk alike; and through it all being yelled at for infractions that we did not yet know were infractions. But here at least, I thought, was to be balm for the tortured soul. Here in the chapel we would receive the spiritual uplift to make the world seem right again.

The chaplain, a middle-aged, corpulent chap, was wearing, not a garment of the Lord, but one of Caesar. He stood before us with his chaplain's insignias gleaming on collars that sat above a chest of combat ribbons. And as he preached his welcoming sermon of "Question not, believe in Him" we were made to understand that the "Him" referred to was our officers and non-coms.

He then smiled benignly and explained that he was there to serve us. He wished us to regard him as our "parent-away-from-home," and that in order to best serve us it was necessary to have as much information about each of us as possible. Therefore, would we please fill out some forms? The forms were passed out to us. And in the dim light of that "holy" place I read such questions as: Did you use to have sexual relations with A) other boys, B) men, C) girls, D) women. Did your father and mother sleep in A) separate rooms, B) the same bed, C) separate beds. The money you have saved amounts to between A) $1.00 and $50.00 B)$50.00 and $200.00 C) $200.00 and $1,000.00 D) If over $1,000.00, specify how much _____ . You keep your savings A) on your person, B) in a bank, C) other. Specify which one _____ , where _____ . You usually get up to urinate A) once a night, B) twice a night, C) not at all after retiring, D) more than twice a night.

We were given a half hour to fill out this outrage-against-our-privacy document and then called into the chaplain's back office individually and alphabetically. Because my name came near the end of the alphabet and because there were dozens of us waiting, it took over two hours of waiting with nothing to do but stare down at our sacred answers. During this time two things happened. The first was that we end-of-the-alphabeters got restless. And so, as in theatres when the film abruptly stops, most of us lifted our voices and whistles in tones of displeasure. Result: the back door was thrown open and the indignant chaplain made it known that we were in the house of the Lord and to act accordingly, which we shamefacedly did. The second thing that occurred was that, the more I reread the form the angrier I became at the intimately personal inquiries. Then, it was decided. I would erase the entire thing. And I did.

In bloated contentment the chaplain sat in the squeaking swivel chair behind the only adornment of his back room, a confession-

like railing. Checking off the next name he called out, ''Tyler,''
and radiating his paternal smile as the door opened, ushering in
another sheep. Casually reaching out for the man's paper, his
baby-blue eyes automatically scanned the page, then stopped
abruptly and began over àgain at the top. The paternal smile
changed to a hard, set line, the close-cropped head shook sideways
in disbelief and he sputtered,

''What do you mean by this, soldier?''

''Sorry, sir, but I thought the questions were kind of personal
. . .''

''Apparently you weren't listening to my lecture. Didn't I just
finish telling you not to question things in the Army?''

''Yes, sir, but. . .''

''Never mind the buts. Get back in that room and fill this thing
out.''

''I'd rather not, sir.''

There was then a long thundering silence. He then looked at the
wall and quietly told me to fill out as much of it as I felt inclined to,
but at least put something down. I did. My name, rank, and serial
number.

Shortly thereafter I applied for OCS. The desk sergeant looked at
me through narrowed, knowing eyes and said, ''Oh yeah, yer
Tyler, aincha? Well, Well, a report on ya from the chaplain has
gone into yer file. We got our eye on yer, Tyler! Oughta be
ashamed of yerself, having been the *ringleader* in that big ruckus
over at the chapel the other night. No, with that report in yer file
ya ain't got a snowball in hell's chance for OCS.''

When I protested that such had not been the case, he coughed
and turned away. Later, many ''odd'' things happened to me,
such as:

During combat in Korea, I received an in-the-field promotion as
acting sergeant, yet despite promises the actual promotion never
went through. And, when put in for the Silver Star medal for
gallantry in action, it went through even to where the Army sent
notification of my having received it to the local newspapers, yet it
was never awarded me publicly as the other men's were, but years
later — through the mail.

I might say that I entered the Army more religious than most. I
attended services most of my youth and sang in the Episcopal choir
for years, however, since that memorable evening in the chapel at
Fort Leonard Wood ''I have never worshipped God.''

The question of whom the chaplain is really working for, his church or
the military establishment, was given some documentation in a 1957 study
of American chaplains. In the sample that was taken, 79 percent of the
chaplains thought that ''a man with good religious training would make a

better soldier than one who lacked such training." And 45 percent believed that "killing of an enemy soldier was a righteous act." The remaining 55 percent called this killing "a justifiable act."[27] One sociologist of religion says the chaplain "performs the shamanic role par excellence — the religious indoctrination of the tribe's warriors as they go out to face the enemy."[28]

Chaplains have helped justify even the killing of Americans, when the military decreed it to be necessary. In the pathetic case of the only American executed for alleged desertion during the twentieth century, a World War II Private Slovik was to be executed by the enlisted men of his own company under order of Commanding General Eisenhower. Some members of the squad did not want to kill a fellow American. One contacted Chaplain Cummings and

> "told him we had tried to get out of the firing squad, but he said we shouldn't feel bad, that the decision had been made by our superiors and that we had a job to do. Father Cummings was the anchor man of the indoctrination team. On January 30, he told them to do their duty . . . that the decision to shoot Slovik was not theirs to question . . . that the responsibility for Slovik's death had been assumed by higher authority. Then, just before the execution procession was to leave the guardroom, Father Cummings talked with Slovik, said mass for him and granted him absolution."[29]

Surprisingly, the American chaplain retains a generally respected role among the public and even in many religious communities. Apparently, the hypocrisy of the chaplain is not clearly understood, and religious communities have not taken the responsibility to provide civilian ministers to administer last rites to soldiers dying from overseas battle. This is possibly the only legitimate function of a chaplain and it could be performed by civilian ecclesiastics working in overseas hospitals, in a role similar to that of members of the Red Cross. The present system not only serves to sanction and therefore encourage war, but the chaplains become corruptors of their own faith by giving priority to the values of their military employer.[30]

The Biblical Commandment, "Thou shalt not *kill*"[31] puts the Christian chaplain in an untenable position, if he gives credence to it. So the Christian Commandments have been *omitted* from the *Armed Forces Hymnal*. Only the Judaic version is included, accompanying the Jewish section. The sixth Commandment is stated "Thou shalt not *murder*." Presumably "murder" can be treated as a legal term and therefore (if one uses the modern legal meaning of murder as violation of the laws of a nation) authorized killing by the military becomes exempt from the crime of murder. Early Christian morality did not base moral authority on secular legality, and this kind of cynical semantic deception only illuminates how chaplains who claim to represent Christian ideals have in fact sold their religious values to serve values mandated as a sin in both Old and New Testaments.

The chaplain's divine sanction of American foreign policy is indeed flattering to the American presidency, since it endows his decisions with holiness higher than that of ordinary mortals. It is reminiscent of the tyranny of the Divine Right of Kings, which was rejected by the American founding fathers. It would make sense in a medieval context to think of cosmic authority justifying the world in which the chaplain lives. By having a Chaplain's Corps, it is easier for the "nobility" who frequent officers' quarters, clubs, and bars, and who both sanction and even arrange for prostitution near bars to assure worried mothers that their sons and daughters are being morally uplifted by their lives as military "serfs." Another reason for the existence of the Chaplain's Corps is that it provides the Pentagon with a public relations device to resist public pressure against suspected military degradation of American youth.

The chaplains are only one group in many who have accommodated themselves to the powerful pressures of an immense system which uses increasingly powerful techniques to persuade and even force conformity and adjustment. In a massive institution committed to violence and killing, many of those who fall within its influence tend to make the intellectual, semantic, emotional, and moral adjustments necessary to serve its goals.

II

INDOCTRINATION AND CONVERSION

A. PR PROPAGANDA

Is the massive economic support the military continues to receive the result of civilian-generated interests? The Constitution requires that the Armed Forces serve civilian policy which emanates from the President as Commander-in-Chief, transmitted through the State Department as foreign policy and implemented through the Department of Defense. This *formal* pattern, however, often bears little relationship to the *informal* processes of decision making. General policy is usually created through the power structure of American politics. The democratic theory of the "American dream" assumes that there is free and open examination of basic issues affecting the nation and that citizens may participate in policy making through their chosen representatives. What actually occurs is usually very different.

Since it is of the nature of bureaucracies to first maintain their own existence, government agencies tend to exaggerate their relative importance. The obsession of the F.B.I. and the C.I.A. with the dangers of subversion is designed, among other things, to guarantee their own institutional growth. When militarists become convinced that they need a larger share of national income and manpower to protect American citizens

14

from the dangers of the larger world, they typically offer an appraisal of national needs from their own limited and possibly self-seeking point of view. The larger the military becomes, however, the more power it has to argue successfully that additional military expansion is needed. The big have special advantage in becoming bigger. In expanding such power, reality is likely to be defined in a manner that supports the power objectives of the expanding institution. *The military, the alleged protector of nations, has a vested interest in seeing that people view the world as one in which militarism is necessary.* Scare announcements from the Pentagon are usually timed to coincide with congressional budget decisions. Exaggerated statements were made of a Chinese nuclear threat to sell the A.B.M., and a similar rigged case was made about the Russian threat, to sell the MIRV system (multiple warheads).[32]

The Armed Forces have developed a massively financed propaganda agency, not primarily to responsibly inform people, but rather to get them to accept conclusions favoring the military. In 1969, there were over 6000 Pentagon public relations men around the world and 339 lobbyists. Fred Cook refers to this as "Madison Avenue in Uniform."[33] He describes in detail how a massive campaign was used after World War II to sell Universal Military Training to the American people. This major tactical offensive of the military worked through a large and expensive public relations staff with cooperation of the largest motion picture studio in the East; through the distribution of thousands of photographic prints each month to newspapers, TV stations, and news-reels; through assistance to numerous commercial film corporations when they presented the "right" image of the military; and through speeches to clubs of all kinds. The target was the American public which, ironically, was picking up the tab. The War Department produced and distributed a film entitled *A Plan for Peace* designed to sell UMT. Military planes carried officers to deliver UMT speeches, and congressmen's desks soon became stacked with pro-UMT material.

No government funds were available for an anti-UMT campaign, and so with this massive campaign, financed with taxpayers' money, the *military* view became highly influential in *political* policy making. In 1948, a year after World War II draft laws had expired, Universal Military Training, accompanied by vast increases in military appropriations, became law. American business was hardly expected to protest, for the lucrative post-war military industrial complex was given birth. However, its existence was not publicly acknowledged until President Eisenhower, upon leaving office *13 years later,* warned against its inordinate influence in American life.

Small voices of protest were heard in government, but they were ineffective. The Harness Committee of the House of Representatives reported that "The War Department followed a pattern unworthy of any Department of Government,"[34] and a military defector from the Pentagon wrote a book because "he was shocked at the Pentagon's ultimate goal of a 10-million-man army, dominated by a professional officer's corps into which virtually no draftee could break."[35] He said that to establish UMT, "The huge professional officer's corps was converted into a propaganda organization, the like of which the world had never seen."

Historians now have an interesting problem to determine to what degree the military influence in manipulating public opinion has *created* the cold war. Obviously, the claim of danger of the Russians was not a complete fabrication. Yet in a continuously precarious world, one must learn to assess danger with a sense of proportion. The military had its special ideological metaphysical, economic, and prestige interests at stake. Its activities helped manipulate the process of political decision making. Yet for many Americans the economic enticements of a huge continuous military establishment were welcomed, and a sizeable number of political-military alliances were formed.

The Presidential campaign of 1948 coincided with the massive UMT campaign of the Pentagon. The opposing Republican party criticized the Democrats for being soft on Communism and supported the Pentagon thesis of peace through military strength. The Democratic reply was to assert that it was not soft on Communism and that it too believed in peace through military strength. When Truman and the Democrats were re-elected, both parties supported UMT. Ever since, both parties have turned the military thesis of peace through military strength into a seemingly perennial orthodoxy, a cornerstone of foreign policy that until the Vietnam debacle produced virtually unanimous bi-partisan support.

Since this fateful episode in the manipulation of ideas, the military has steadily *increased* its "communications" network. It boasts proudly of 240 radio and television stations in over 32 countries. It also sponsors civilian radio newscasts, a way of using public funds to make unfavorable news releases about the military less likely.

A publication of the Armed Forces says that "newspapers, radio, public speaking, and television were once strange and disturbing elements to the military. Today, they are tools of leadership placed at the commander's disposal by the information officer."[36] The obvious problem in all this is that there is a conflict of interest, for the military with an official ideological outlook is no more likely to be a source of objective reporting than *Pravda.* the official Russian publication. Each has a preconceived view of the world, each has journalists with a vested interest in job security, and each lives in an institutional subculture with its own special outlook. Each would be disappointed if the world did not turn out to be the way it was claimed to be. Information given to the American people bears an important relationship to public policy formation and to the course of action which will determine the world of tomorrow, if there is to be one. Armed Forces information claims to describe reality. It also creates it.

Successful propaganda seldom uses such crude techniques as the big

lie. Instead the factual information offered may be scrupulously *exact.*
Clueing in meaning, *classifying* events, and *selecting* materials can move
the reader toward accepting the desired conclusion. Propaganda is increasingly created not so much by *distortion as by omission,* by not including what does not fit the preconceptions. Armed Forces information
officers include many people who try to do a responsible job, but Armed
Forces "information" is an instrument of support for defense policy and is
unlikely to stand outside and be critical of that very policy.

The influence of the Pentagon in creating a military-oriented foreign
policy still persists, though not as obviously as in 1948. The military is able
to participate in defining international "reality" and thus influence
American foreign policy. The Pentagon alliance, with selected
congressmen, industrialists, and journalists provides enormous power to
sell the Pentagon product. In 1965, the Joint Chiefs-of-Staff broke with
their Secretary of Defense to lobby and campaign for their plan for a
"thick" ABM system.[37] Fred Cook claims that "The crutch of the
Warfare State is propaganda. We must be taught to fear and to hate or we
will not agree to regiment our lives, to bear the enormous burdens of
heavier taxations, to pay for ever more costly military hardware."[38]

B. THE MILITARY MIND

Studies by social-psychologists have shown relationships between
ideology and personality types. Adorno's (et. al.) study of *The
Authoritarian Personality* and Rokeach's *The Open and Closed Mind* have
been particularly useful in identifying some of these relationships. Adorno
found that there is a close correlation between the view that the world
revolves around one's own "in group" (ethnocentrism) and what is ordinarily called a conservative political-economic outlook. "Ethnocentrism
is based on a pervasive and rigid in-group out-group distinction; it involves
stereotyped negative imagery and hostile attitudes regarding out-groups . . .
and a hierarchical, authoritarian view of group interaction in which in-
groups are rightly dominant, out-groups subordinate."[39]

Adorno has found that the ethnocentric-authoritarian individual
shows special susceptibility to Fascist ideology. Such ideology apparently
provides a view of the world and particular need gratification necessary to
the maintenance of this personality pattern. The pattern is characterized by
suspicion, a belief that human nature is inherently warlike, and fantasies
about "secret plots which control our lives."[40]

Other characteristics include a "moralistic facade" with an absence of
inner guilt, since the inner self and personal ethical values are underdeveloped. There is dependency on strong leadership and a sense of
personal weakness which is tied up with fears of nonmasculinity. Four
characteristics are common: 1. Power-strivings, 2. Toughness, 3. Flight
into heterosexual activity, and 4. Paranoid reactions. This latent fear of
personal weakness often expresses itself in exalted notions of "will power,
discipline, determination" and an exaggerated sense of "honor."[41]

17

The pattern of the non-authoritarian and largely unprejudiced person is very different. Such people

> seek above all love — which they have some capacity to give. Despite frustration and conflict their approach to life is influenced by basic respect for themselves and other people. This makes for democratic identifications with other people, and for inclination to identify with underdogs.[42]

In the authoritarian personality, there is great difficulty in perceiving the world with any accuracy, for "people who have the greatest difficulty in facing themselves are the least able to see the way the world is made."[43]

Milton Rokeach's study of *The Open and Closed Mind* points out, as does Adorno, the way in which cognitive processes, personality styles, and ideology are related. When one factor is known, the other is capable of some degree of prediction. Rokeach claims that *what* you believe is not as crucial as *how* you believe, a conclusion which would make subcultural influences on attitudes and thought processes more important than explicit ideological instruction. It is of interest that on Rokeach's scale of the "closed mind" one of the main items is "I will try to follow a program of life based on duty," which is crucial to the military creed. Adorno's "F" scale includes items which identify Fascist values. Discriminating items which are of particular interest because they typify the military outlook are:

1. "Obedience and respect for authority are the most important virtues children should learn."
2. "What the youth needs is strict discipline, rugged determination, and the will to work and fight for family and country."
3. "Human nature being what it is, there will always be war and conflict."[44]

It is apparent that the ideology of military tradition corresponds closely with personality correlates of authoritarianism, Fascism, and closed-mindedness, as described by these two leading studies. The sociology of the military also reveals a close correspondence between the military way of life and these authoritarian values.

The correspondence is by no means one to one throughout all phases of military life, however. There are central value patterns to military systems, but there is also a range of variation not only between individual soldiers, but also between branches of the service.

Adorno's "F" (Fascist) scale has been used to determine if military experience actually produces a higher Fascist-authoritarian index. The findings are not uniformly consistent. One problem in such research is that within the larger military establishment there is sufficient variation so that sampling one group makes it difficult to generalize about every other branch of the Armed Forces.

One study of the effects of a year of Air Force training showed authoritarian *reduction*.[45] Janowitz suggests that combat flight training is a special type of military experience which emphasizes "group inter-dependence" and a "team concept of coordination."[46] If his explanation is correct, this is an example of a sub-group within the larger military structure which emphasizes cooperative values more than autocratic values.

Most studies, sampling other areas of the military, have found shifts toward authoritarianism. In a study of Army basic training, Christie found a relationship between acceptance by others within military training groups and shifts toward authoritarianism during training.[47]

Hollander found that Naval Cadets *expected* military leadership to be authoritarian but that those *they* considered to be good leaders were low in authoritarian characteristics.[48]

It is somewhat hazardous to generalize about the few studies of authoritarianism and military behavior, but available evidence suggests the following:

1. Authoritarian values are dominant in all three areas of the military: ideology, behavior, and institutional structure.
2. There is less tight consistency in the value pattern of military behavior than in military ideology and institutional structure.
3. Authoritarian procedures in the military are based primarily on military habit and tradition, unsupported by experimental evidence of the functional value of such procedures.
4. Experimental evidence suggests that soldiers who have spent most of their lives in civilian America would be likely to perform better in an environment which is less authoritarian than what is usually demanded by the American military.[49]
5. The persistence of a traditional structure has made the authoritarian trainee more adapted to the military establishment than a non-authoritarian trainee.[50]

Militarists are often hostile to the suggestion that there is a "military mind." But it is partly this very lack of awareness of his own social psychology which is part of what characterizes the model military type. To the extent that a man is conditioned to believe in the mythology of the military subculture, he becomes a reliable cog in the war-making machine, but he also loses his identity as a person and as a member of a democratic society. To the degree that he has learned to think and behave militarily, he has also learned to accept an autocratic system and ethnocentric-nationalistic values. He is uncritically obedient and duty-oriented, tending toward closed-mindedness and rigidity of belief. His military mind is virtually antithetical to the characteristics needed for a democratic society.

III

THE MILITARY MACHINE-A MASSIVE BUREAUCRACY

A. THE PARKINSONIAN GOLIATH

In the view of Morris Janowitz, a sociologist of military behavior, the major difference between the military establishment and other American institutions "derives from the requirement that its members are specialists in making use of violence and mass destruction . . . . military mission is the key to military organization."[51]

Another highly visible characteristic of the American military establishment is its size. It is a bureaucratic structure, increasingly multiplying its administrative processes with the rules and directives which descend from "above." It might be considered the archetype of fully functioning Parkinson's Law, where "work expands to fill the time available." C. Wright Mills described the mammoth Pentagon bureaucracy as follows:

The world's largest office building, the United States Capitol, would fit neatly into any one of its five segments. Three football fields would reach only the length of one of its five outer walls. Its seventeen and a half miles of corridor, 40,000 phone switchboards, fifteen miles of pneumatic tubing, 2,100 intercoms, connect with one another and with the world, the 31,300 Pentagonians. Prowled by 170 security officers, served by 1,000 men and women, it has four full-time workers doing nothing but replacing light bulbs, and another four watching the master panel which synchronizes its 4,000 clocks.[52]

The military has a hierarchy of power, authority and status based largely on a two-class social system drawn from the feudal ages. Officers try to retain the status equivalent of the nobility, while enlisted men are forced into the role paralleling the serf. One sociologist classifies the American military establishment as "feudal-bureaucratic."[53]

Both Mills and Janowitz claim that World War II was a major turning point for the American military establishment, for during and since the early 1940's the military establishment has become more interconnected with the economic, political, social, and educational segments of American society. Since 1950, over half of the total federal budget has been allocated to the military, even though the size of the total budget has continually increased. The rate of the increase is indicated in the following figures:[54]

Year	National Defense Costs in Billions [55]
1930	.7
1935	.7
1940	1.5
1945	81.3
1946	43.3
1948	11.8
1950	13.0
1952	44.0
1954	47.0
1956	40.7
1958	44.2
1960	45.7
1961	47.5
1962	51.1
1963	52.8
1964	54.2
1965	50.2
1966	56.8
1967	70.1
1968	80.5
1969	81.0
1970	81.5

The continuous infusion of military spending into the economy provides large profits for certain industries, often from contracts which are not subject to competitive bidding. The convenient arrangement between industry and the military is not likely to disappear even if peace should break out. While industry's chief executives such as Charles Wilson and Robert McNamara became Secretaries of Defense presiding over massive expenditures, the retired militarists in turn were welcomed into industry at levels of authority commensurate with the contribution they were able to make in getting further military contracts. General Lucius Clay was made Chairman of the Board at Continental Can Company, General James Doolittle became Vice President of Shell Oil Company, General Omar Bradley became Board Chairman of Bulova Research Laboratories, and General Douglas MacArthur was made Chairman of the Board of Remington Rand. [56] Industry has known what constitutes the necessary "talent" of top executives in a warfare state, and the public has shown little concern for this new kind of interlocking directorate. Unions have often joined the power elite and helped send congressmen to Washington to secure a share of the military pie for labor. With such vested interests in the cold war, it is most unlikely that anything short of national fear of nuclear annihilation from an unnecessary arms race will cause the thriving military hierarchy to be substantially reduced.

B. THE TOTAL WELFARE STATE

Except for its economic dependence on the larger society, the American military establishment is a highly self-contained sub-society that has developed womb-to-tomb provisions. A child born in a military hospital, delivered by a military doctor, may attend military "dependent's schools," live with his family in military housing, eat food from the commissary, and go to post theaters and libraries. Later, he may attend a military academy and as an officer be surrounded with even more ubiquitous military influences until the day he is buried in a military cemetery with the rites offered by a military chaplain. Russia and China provide a close parallel to this total institutional life combining total welfare with a similar lack of democratic freedom. This is an ironic aspect of the American military system for the totalitarian aspects of Communism, which it so fanatically opposes, are in many ways similar to the American military system itself. The stated goals are different, but the use of a planned elitist system is the same. The relationship of the individual to the system is also comparable to the extent that each system controls and defines the meaning of the individual's life; both are totalitarian.

For the American military, the characteristics of this total society can be classified as:

1. A total, isolated institution including provisions for work, play, eating, sleeping, worship, education, and burial. Symbolic arrangements also foster isolation from the larger community.
2. An organizational identity which includes total identification with the required roles.
3. An esoteric profession which includes the sacred and the mystical, particularly in connection with ceremony about violence and the state.
4. A hierarchical organization where power and status are clearly defined.
5. A class-status system based on traditions of caste.
6. An ethos and ideology which permeate the establishment. [57]

The term "military mind," though usually rejected by the military, is the personality structure compatible with this organic value-permeated environment. In the same way that the Hopi Indians are what they are, through special cultural experience, so members of the American military are influenced by the special characteristics of their subculture. Yet, two qualifications need to be made to this generalization.

First, American military characteristics are not unlike some aspects of American civilian institutions, particularly large corporations. Second, those who enter the military are not always altered in the direction of military values. Some remain unscathed, others react in opposition. The person who adapts to the military often sees in it an environment that meets some of his special needs. The tough, aggressive image of the Marine Corps provides an opportunity for many volunteers to act out such tendencies.

However, for the child who is raised in the military and continues to live in this environment, there is little chance that his outlook will be unaffected. For those who enter the military for any substantial period of time, the ubiquitous influences are likely to create a disciple of military values. This is especially likely for a young person whose identity is still quite indeterminate. Even for most adults in our "other-directed" society, there are few defenses against such pervasive value transmission.

C. THE NEW LOOK

Post-Korean publications of the Armed Forces refer to the "new" military and the "modern" military. The impression is given that the military has substantially changed in recent years.[58] It has undergone some changes, but they have been primarily in equipment and secondary functions rather than in structure.

Minor changes were made after World War II, but the rate of basic change before then was hardly dramatic. In 1943, Colonel Thomas R. Phillips said that Army regulations on discipline remained unchanged in all essential respects from those of 1821, and those were copied from the regulations of the noble and peasant army of royal France of 1788.[59] After World War II, major attempts at structural reform were made by the Doolittle Board, which was created by the Secretary of War to investigate enlisted man-officer relationships and to recommend improvements. The study revealed that social distinctions between enlisted men and officers were most resented.[60] Enlisted man-officer inequalities in pay, food, housing, uniforms, etc., were the next most resented by enlisted men.

Extensive hearings and much discussion finally resulted in minor changes. Social separation (military apartheid) between officers and enlisted men was eased by such changes as eliminating saluting *outside* military installations, except in occupied territories. Separate officer's clubs and athletic facilities were continued on a traditional "separate but equal" basis. Spindler, in his study of the results of the board, concluded that the results are one more indication that "no fundamental changes in the structure of command and the previously established lines of communications are to be tolerated."[61] Changes that could have produced structural revision were carefully held in check (such as having enlisted men tried by a jury of their peers instead of by the caste above them). Enlisted men were made eligible to sit in a court-martial when it was requested by the accused, but officers continued to retain majority control.

Other minor reforms have occurred, but most of the changes have resulted from new technology and the shifts in role from the total defeat objectives of World War II to the holding operation goals of Korea. The more complicated technology of the newer weapons have resulted in an increase in specialists, particularly in the Air Force, with some effect on traditional procedures. Janowitz points out that "the coordination of a group of specialists cannot be guaranteed simply by authoritarian discipline."[62] Military authority has had some tendency, therefore, to "shift from reliance on practices based on domination to a wider utilization of manipulation . . . Domination involves threats and negative sanctions rather than positive incentives. It tends to produce mechanical compliance. Manipulation involves influencing an individual's behavior less by giving explicit instructions and more by indirect techniques of group persuasion and by emphasis on group goals.[63]

The increased use of manipulation rather than fear of punishment now occurs primarily through the use of ideological indoctrination and group pressures. Janowitz's review of the reason for the post-Korean emphasis on ideological indoctrination deserves quoting:

> (A U.S. Senate Committee) paid no attention to the extensive defections of the Communists experienced when voluntary repatriation took place. It overlooked the inherent limitations of resistance to Communist tactics by a partially mobilized armed force of a political democracy, and understated the actual extent of correct behavior by American troops . . . It recommended ideological indoctrination, rather than suggesting changes in administrative and training procedures which would produce more effective military forces. The effect of civilian and congressional criticism was to strengthen those elements in the military profession who held that the armed forces should have a broad educational function.

> As part of the absolutist orientation of the reorganized Joint Chiefs of Staff, (Admiral) Radford authorized the "implementation" of a "program of Evaluation and Assessment of Freedom," entitled "Militant Liberty."[64]

The Air Force, with its commitment to absolutist military doctrine and its sensitivity toward public relations activities, reacted most ambitiously in the search for an ideology, while the older services were more resistant to such efforts. It instituted a variety of programs, almost devoid of historical reference and centering on the glorification of air power.[65]

The Air Force issued regulations directing itself to "the difficult task of trying to build back the true sense of values the country once had." The Air Force decreed that "in this immediate aim of re-educating the country in its basic beliefs, the military services had an opportunity to make a significant contribution — re-education of the serviceman."[66]

The branches of the Armed Forces which make less use of the technical specialist and more use of the combat group, such as the Army and the Marine Corps, have given more attention to manipulation through group psychology than through ideology. Though manipulation is by no means democratic, it is more subtle and therefore appears less dehumanizing than the older forms of domination. Being less obvious, it may be even more nefarious.

New recruits have traditionally been subjected to procedures based on the concept of shock treatment — an abrupt, even traumatic transfer into the rigors of military life without any transition from civilian life. World War II research and later studies, especially those of the Korean War, have focused more attention on group morale and survival motivation. It was found in Korea that when Americans were willing to fight, it was often because they were defending a buddy.[67] This suggests that love is a more powerful motive than hate. Since then, the military has grotesquely made use of this kill-for-love strategy by keeping combat units together and encouraging soldiers to shoot to kill to save their buddies.

It was also found that most of the American servicemen, who collaborated with the enemy in Korea, came from units which "had not developed high social cohesion."[68] Training has therefore shifted more in the direction of techniques aimed at group persuasion and troop participation.

There is comparatively little research which identifies the actual effectiveness and the *human* consequences of military training. There is a serious question about the value of traditional conceptions of military training either for military objectives or for the larger purpose of a democratic society.[69] The use of positive incentives and learning by problem-solving is showing the same superior results in the military, when it is used, as it has in industry and education. Yet, fear of punishment and conditioned-response regimentation still dominate as a teaching method. When semi-democratic processes are introduced, they produce tensions and conflict in the traditional military structure. Since the "modern" military has managed to pass beyond sabers, epaulets, and dueling (though not entirely beyond swagger sticks), it is possible that social and psychological research could lead to fundamental revision of military training and military life. The results might be used to produce radical changes in current pre-scientific conceptions of human behavior which underlie much military thinking. Or on the other hand, research may lead only to increased effectiveness of indoctrination and conditioning without altering traditional military values.

Marching, drilling, parading, saluting, and spit-and-polish inspections are still very much a part of military life. The rigidity and ceremonialism of military tradition continues in spite of some changes produced by increased bureaucratization, increased use of technicians, and increased evidence of the need for structural revision. Janowitz concedes that there may continue to be one use for ceremonialism in the military, namely, "a device for dealing with the fear of death." However, he also claims that though "nostalgia for the past expresses itself in increased

25

ceremonialism . . . much of the ceremony seems to be a device for avoiding concern with unsolved problems of military management.''[70],[71]

Military systems are designed to wage war, but they also reflect characteristics based on tradition and on the current cultural-economic-political system. In the American system, the Armed Forces have become burgeoning bureaucracies interwoven with the larger society, especially with industries which profit from military contracts. Militarists are sufficiently in contact with the larger society so that they do not constitute a group with characteristics entirely different from civilian society. But they have developed a subculture which emphasizes special characteristics, most of them antithetical to democratic values. The military system is highly autocratic, elitist, and in many ways totalitarian. It most strongly attracts people who have these characteristics, and it has evidenced considerable success in converting the values of trainees.

Since military institutions have as their primary goal the organization and management of violence, the military mission guides many related behavioral patterns. Toughness, aggressiveness, and insensitivity are encouraged, and killing in combat is rationalized by a complex set of processes. Enemy-psychology is developed to dehumanize a designated enemy, and theological sanction aided by the chaplain's corps is used to justify killing. Black and white moral classifications are usually used to define alternatives. The world is described through such choices as free world and slave world, right and wrong, friend and enemy, we and they. In combat, a self-righteous ethnocentrism intensifies hatred and encourages vengeance and atrocities, particularly when the ''enemy'' kills the close friends of a soldier. Since this occurs on both sides, hatred, vengeance, and atrocity escalate during combat.

The American military system influences the larger civilian society by interpreting events through its own value system. When it reports during a war or makes pronouncements on national defense, it does so with the self-interest of the military system in mind. Military power, therefore, creates the kind of social order which supports military values. The continuous influence of a large military system during the last twenty-five years has infused civilian values with military thinking. Formal controls over the military have too often been inadequate; but regardless of what *formal* civilian controls are developed, the pervasive *informal* influences of a massive military system will distort the larger society. In a fascist nation this influence reinforces the social order. In a society which prizes democratic values, it can be catastrophic to the value system. In a world where uncontrolled military power can lead to World War III, catastrophe can involve more than merely a *way* of life.

CHAPTER II

INDOCTRINATING MILITARY IDEOLOGY

Man has a long history of warfare involving a variety of organizations, strategies, and weapons, yet soldiers guiding the ancient legions of Rome shared some common values with modern militarists. The weapons of war have changed faster than the military outlook. This outlook has included, according to one military historian, an emphasis on ''permanence, irrationality, weakness, and evil in human nature. It stresses the supremacy of society over the individual and the importance of order, hierarchy, and division of function. It accepts the . . . continuing likelihood of war.''[1]

Modern armies are immersed in military traditions drawn from centuries past. Prior to the nineteenth century, armies and navies were comprised mainly of impressed seamen, mercenaries and aristocrats. Armies served both predatory and defensive purposes and were supported by the monarchies to serve their special interests. During the nineteenth century, nations developed a permanent officers corps dedicated to the management of violence, and military academies were created to develop the art, science, and philosophy of warfare.

Karl Von Clausewitz established the dominant point of view of modern institutionalized militarism. His nineteenth century writing continues to be quoted by modern military leaders throughout the world. War to Clausewitz became the pursuit of politics by other means — the other means being the use of organized violence. War became the power of the state to compel the acceptance of its will. He asserted the familiar dictum of modern America that the military is purely an instrument to serve non-military political purposes.

But is the American military system merely an instrument? To understand the complex value connections between the military and civilian areas of American society it is useful to examine the value system of the military establishment. Though many specific military characteristics are shared with the larger society, some military functions and traditions provide patterns which are distinctive from civilian institutions.

Professional militarists are technicians whose skills are largely usable to serve any political system, whether it be democratic, communist, or fascist. Those who use the services of the militarist usually honor him, for he is presumed to be serving a good cause. The good cause becomes good from the view point of the user. Since applied militarism results in the killing of human beings and the destruction of human works it is honored by those who favor the mission and equally hated by those who consider the mission to be unjustified. But in the military view, the assigned end is presumed to justify the means.

Specialists in violence require complicated management procedures in this age of science and technology, yet the new demands are accommodated within old traditions. War integrates and expands the military by giving reality and purpose to the military ideology. Peace is boring and deprives the professional soldier of a sense of purpose. In time of peace, display and ceremony become more common, whether or not they have any relationship to the ostensible military goal of efficiently applying violence. When ritualistic activity increases, elaborate rationalization is developed to justify the ritual.

To understand militarism, it is not only useful to identify what is actually done in military establishments; it is also useful to identify the reasons given for what is done. The stated reasons constitute the official goals; they provide a pattern of official military values. In the American armed forces, there is not merely one system of official values. There are at least three.

Each of the three value patterns constitutes a set of beliefs about human nature and society which are in effect ideologies. The various ideologies stem from (1) **general military traditions,** (2) **the national context,** and (3) **the current problems** facing the American establishment. The ideology of traditional militarism is shared largely by militarists in other countries. But the second ideology includes selected features from national culture which are designed to demonstrate that the military serves the values of the nation. The third ideology is subject to change, for it is designed to justify a particular war. This latter ideology may be transmitted from the government that the military is serving yet often the special outlook of those immersed in a military subculture will produce its own special version of ''why we fight.'' The justification is usually in terms that make the most sense to those who have taken on the values of the military establishment.

Documentation of these three American armed forces ideologies will be classified under: (1) Traditions, (2) Selective identification with the larger culture, and (3) Justifications for a particular war. Documentary statements are drawn from post-Korean Armed Forces publications, mainly those of the so-called ''modern'' military of the last decade. They constitute explicit statements of official military values.

IDEOLOGY BASED ON MILITARY TRADITION

The following statements are representative of the pattern of values which constitutes one strand of ideology, centering around traditions and codes of military behavior. Italics have been added to emphasize the more revealing words. The Army **Military Training** manual lists ''discipline'' as the major goal of military training.2 Discipline is described as:

The state of individual and group **training that create a mental attitude** resulting in correct conduct and **automatic obedience** to military law under all conditions. It is founded on respect for, loyalty to, military law and authority. This training is continuous throughout military service . . . Its principles are applied in every military activity. Although it is developed primarily through military drills and repetitive training, every feature of military life has its effect upon military discipline. It is indicated in the individual or unit by smartness of appearance and action; by cleanliness and neatness of dress, equipment and quarters; by respect for seniors; and by the prompt and willing execution by subordinates of both the spirit and intent of orders by instruction.[3]

This is one particular conception of discipline. It does not emphasize self-discipline; rather it emphasizes the development of uncritical conditioned responses to the demand of one's "superior." The "disciplined" soldier has "automatic obedience," and all of military life is said to aim at creating this kind of behavior.

The manual on **Military Leadership** defines "leadership" as "The art of influencing and directing men in such a way as to obtain their **willing obedience, confidence,** respect, and loyal cooperation in order to accomplish the mission."[4] The word "willing" is not included a few pages later when leadership is redefined as "understanding, predicting, and controlling their behavior."[5]

It is also stated that a good leader helps the soldier adjust to Army life. The soldier is adjusted when "he accepts these goals as his own, realizes they are also the Army's goals, and strives to achieve them."[6]

A good leader must instill loyalty. "Loyalty is the quality of faithfulness to country, the Army, your unit, your seniors, subordinates, and associates."[7] A leader should "know, understand, and apply the principles of war"[8] and "teach belief in the cause and mission."[9]

A good leader will "make use of ceremonies, symbols, slogans, and military music." And he will "use competition to develop teamwork," and "make proper use of decorations and awards."[10]

He is also obedient to the "chain of command," for "once the commander has announced his decision of policy, the staff officer must wholeheartedly and enthusiastically support the decision and not allow personal feelings to interfere with the accomplishment of the task."[11] This procedure will work well if the training has been adequate, for **"training will teach the soldier to respond from force of habit** to specific battle orders."[12]

The training should also instill the "Spirit of the offensive" by "the **creation of a desire to close with and destroy the enemy."** This requirement calls for the need to **"instill in men an aggressive attitude."** And leaders should **"set the example** they desire their men emulate."[13]

Clearly, the leader, himself obedient to the higher command, is considered a good leader when he gets those below him to obey. This involves getting the soldier adjusted to the life and the goals of the military so that he responds rapidly and enthusiastically, and with personal dedication, to killing the enemy. The good leader is a model of the values he is trying to inculcate.

The Armed Forces Officer manual was written for officers in all branches of the Armed Forces as "a guide to the philosophy, ideals, and principles of leadership in the United Armed Forces." It states that "within the military establishment the inculcation of ideals is considered the most vital of all teaching."14 Ideals suggested include the system of privilege involved in the two-class officer-enlisted men system. However, unlike the medieval European armies, caste and class is not inherited. But "privilege should attend merit . . . and is a reward for effort and enterprise."15 Once obtained, an example of privilege would be that "normally, an officer is not expected to stand in a chow line, or any other queue in line of duty. The presumption is that his time is more valuable to the Service than that of an enlisted man."16

This book includes a chapter on "human nature" and another on "group nature." The point of view does not refer to any research in the social or behavioral sciences, nor to different philosophical conceptions. Rather "documentation" is made by quoting previous militarists and citing examples from previous battles. Man is said to possess "instinct," but also "plasticity," which permits military training to triumph over instinct. "The heterogeneous crowd is swayed by the voice of instinct. Properly trained, any military unit, being a homogeneous body, should be swayed by the voice of training. Out of uniformity of environment comes uniformity of character and spirit."17 For example, "There is only one correct way to wear the uniform. When any deviations in dress are condoned within the Services, the way is open to destruction of all uniformity and unity."18

It is made clear here that the traditions of the military, such as wearing a uniform, are part of a procedure which aims at reducing uniqueness and individuality. The total transformation is considered to be possible because of human plasticity. Complete adaptation of thought and behavior is to be made to the military environment. The new identity of the soldier is based entirely on the external patterns of symbolism and procedure which is prescribed by the military and rooted in military tradition.

Though many military publications incessantly state that there is no basic difference between the military and the larger American way of life,19 The Armed Forces Officer asserts that there is. It says, "The relation of the military establishment to American democracy is that of a shield covering the body . . . An officer is not only an administrator but a magistrate, and it is this dual role that makes his function so radically different from anything encountered in civil life." The military is a "new way of life" which is not democratic, and it would be injured if it became more democratic. "Authority is questioned in democratic countries today, not only in government, but in industry, the school, the church, and the home. But to the extent that military men lose their faith in its virtue and become amenable to ill-considered reform simply to appease the public, they relinquish the power to protect and nurture that growth of free men, free thought, and free institutions."[20]

This remarkable and ironic statement shows thorough dissociation of the military from democratic values, even though the democratic values of the larger society are given as the cause deserving military protection. Military tradition is apparently assumed to be an autonomous law in itself which should supersede public authority. The voice of the public is clearly suspect and to be resisted. The inference is that people do not know what is best for them.

The characteristics of the "authority" which should be accepted are not made clear, but the statement seems to say that not questioning is the process by which the military can protect a free society. What is really meant by freedom is also not clear, but questioning and freedom do not deem to be connected. However, it is clearly stated that the military gains its strength by not questioning. "No man can make it a wholly 'democratic' institution in its process without vitiating its strength, since it progresses through the exercise of unquestioned authority at various levels."[21]

While belief in "democracy" is considered a hindrance to a military establishment, "patriotism" to one's country is considered essential.[22] It is also necessary that a soldier "puts aside the banner of individuality for that of obedience."[23] Yet this is by no means a sacrifice that causes man to lose more than he gains. Quite the opposite, for it is said to provide more personal reward than any other kind of life. "Than the Service, there is no other environment more conducive to the leading of the full life . . . "[24]

At this point the military is not considered to be merely a "shield" protecting civilian democracy. The military is considered the highest form of life. The ethnocentric militarist appears to have defined his nation through his own value system and found his nation wanting, while militarism has become the ideal. This is flatly contradictory to the official civilian view that the American military is purely an instrument to protect the larger society.

The job of the officer is, therefore, not simply to prepare men to fight. It includes inducting them into a way of life and altering them as human beings from their previous, presumably less perfect condition. A leader "is directed to center his effort primarily on the building of good character in other individuals."[25] The meaning of this "good" character is based on the military value system, which emphasizes "obedience as a moral quality."[26] It emphasizes man's "plastic and impressionable nature, . . . his marked ability to adjust to any enviroment."[27] It also encourages some Spartan elements of self-denial, "To be temperate in all things, to be content, and to refrain from loose living of any sort."[28] Also, "Within the military establishment the inculcation of ideals is considered the most vital of all teaching . . . They influence the personal life and conduct of millions of men who move in and out of the Services, they have regenerative effect upon the spiritual fiber of the Nation as a whole."[29] The ideals are military ideals, and we again see here that there is a belief in the inherent rightness, even superiority of military values over all others, not simply as means but also ends.

Human nature is conceived in such a way that it is believed that only force will produce order. "If all military power were stricken tomorrow, men would revert to a state of anarchy." Political advice is also given, that we must in our time believe that "The main hope is that peace-loving nations will be strong enough to discourage would-be aggressors from launching a war."[30] National military power is therefore advocated as our main hope for peace.

Traditional military beliefs are based on the certainty that they are grounded in absolute truth. Human nature is considered to be fixed and unchanging, and the militarist is certain that he has the correct view of human nature and social order. He allows only one meaning of basic terms. "Discipline" becomes automatic obedience; "leadership" is the capacity to achieve discipline; "authority" is the demand of one's superiors within the hierarchical system. The military outlook, based on the certainty that its way is the right way, becomes not only a way of life, but is assumed to be the highest form of living. It therefore justifies pronouncements on virtually all human problems, even political problems. The military view of the world is unequivocally offered as the only view on which society and international order can be based.

TRADITIONAL VALUES CLASSIFIED

Most traditional military values are common to military establishments of all countries regardless of political ideology. There have been minor changes in these values since the Middle Ages, particularly in the way the American two-class military system has become more open than in the feudal period. Yet the "good" soldier is still aggressive in battle, obedient to orders, and well-disciplined to conform to military authority. He defines himself in relation to military values and identifies with the military establishment. He plays down individuality and plays up uniformity. Patriotism has a religious aura and reverence. Those whom the state labels "the enemy" become the enemy of the soldier, and he is ready to destroy the enemy even at the risk of his life. He does not simply offer his services to an institution, he is expected to give his life psychologically and physically. Military traditions emphasize that the goals of a man's life should not be developed by him; rather, they should be uncritically accepted from military traditions. The military establishment is presumed not only to have a right but even an obligation to prescribe the values in which soldiers should believe. The soldier is presumed to become free by

32

doing what he ought to do and by believing what he ought to believe. This "ought" is based on military values. The soldier's personality and even his views as to the meaning of reality should be militarily controlled, reputedly for the good of the country and also for the good of the soldier.

This pattern of belief constitutes an ideology. As with most ideologies, it is partly rational, but like a secular religion it is taken largely on faith and represents a tightly held belief that is not likely to be open to criticism. Ideologies may become self-conscious social philosophies, but typically they are absolutistic dogmas which provide "answers" to the meaning of human nature, society, economics, government, and correct human behavior.

The value system of most American military traditions corresponds with the ideology of **totalitarianism.** It is, in fact, a totalitarian system within a larger governmental framework which professes to be democratic. The term "totalitarian" usually refers only to government. A totalitarian state is thought to be one which has virtually total control over the individual. But ideology can embrace more than the relationship between man and government. It is useful here to use the term "totalitarian" to include any relationship which aims at total control in the sense that an individual's life is controlled and largely defined by an external source.

A totalitarian value system tries to define human characteristics through external control in such a manner that a person uncritically accepts any imposed pattern of behavior and belief. The individual is encouraged to accept control without being selective, to follow the conclusions of an external authority. Totalitarian "freedom" involves doing and believing what is prescribed, without using judgment to question and to come to one's own conclusion.

The two leading totalitarian **political** doctrines are communism and fascism. Communism is a theory of historical determinism which assumes that there is inevitable social progress based on class conflict. The oppressed class will create a non-exploitative society which will utilize the individual abilities of people and distribute wealth according to individual need. The means to achieve a communist society have included the use of a totalitarian elite employing many of the power characteristics of fascism as a means to move toward socialistic goals.

Fascism is a theory of power in which might makes right and the strong are considered morally justified to rule the weak. Domination by a power elite is therefore normal. Order and uniformity are ends in themselves, and the Nation State is an object of reverence. Fascist citizens have a duty to serve the elitist-controlled State and to display loyalty. They are rewarded if they do and punished if they do not. Modern fascism demands that each citizen be a specialist, contributing to the industrial or military power of the state.

In any totalitarian system, effective criticism of the assumptions underlying the system cannot be tolerated. Orthodoxy and heresy are sharply defined, and though intelligence may be developed to strengthen the system, it must not attempt to alter the system.

It is clear that traditional military values fit the totalitarian classification. Since the military ideal is hierarchical and not equalitarian, it is closer to fascism than to communism. This means that the value compatibility between military establishments and fascist governments is very high, while the general totalitarian outlook of the military tradition and a communist system provides some basis for compatibility. However, the compatibility between military values and democratic values is minimal. In fact, they fundamentally conflict at many points. Therefore it is a special ideological challenge for the American Armed Forces to reconcile military values to the professed values of the larger society, for the ideals of American democracy are claimed to be neither fascist nor communist, presumably opposed to all forms of totalitarianism.

IDEOLOGY BASED ON IDENTIFICATION WITH THE LARGER CULTURE

Military publications not only support the ideology of military traditions but also contain ideology which seeks to justify the military establishment within the larger culture. This ideology is designed to give the soldier patriotic identification with what are assumed to be the fundamental values of his country. It also serves to persuade the civilians that the military establishment supports their values.

American society and its traditions are pluralistic and difficult to contain within a tight ideological system. Yet the Americanism of military ideology is tight and consistent, and therefore represents **selected** ideas from the total American scene, even though military publications make no admission to this fact.

The early American conceptions of liberty, at least as they appear in popular lore, are cited repeatedly to illustrate the preferred ideology. An ideological guide to Armed Forces instructors titled **The Battle for Liberty** shows that there is not only a preferred ideology, but a preferred theology as well:

We believe that an individual has rights, privileges, and responsibilities because **he is a child of God**. We recognize the existence of good and bad — **a basic moral law in nature**. We believe that any government established by man should be based on these basic moral laws and a recognition of the dignity of man as a child of God.[31]

This theologically sanctioned conception of morality underlying American government is common in Armed Forces materials. In **The U.S. Fighting Man's Code** it is stated that "faith will triumph," and one of the articles in the code states "I will trust in my God and in the United States of America."[32] The Declaration of Independence is quoted to give support to the theistic sanctions of the military ideology: We hold these **truths to**

34

be self-evident, that all men are created equal, that they are endowed by their Creator with certain unalienable Rights, that among these are Life, Liberty and the pursuit of Happiness. That to secure these rights, Governments are instituted among Men, deriving their just powers from the consent of the governed ... '' [33]

God is presumed to be on the side of the American soldier, and he is asked to "trust in God" and told that "Men who recognize the existence of God and believe in the importance of a man's soul recognize also that there are worse things than death; as a result, the idea of death does not appall them ... When death ends this earthly struggle it opens the door to everlasting life." The front of the pamphlet includes a quotation from Thomas Jefferson saying "resistance to tyrants, obedience to God," and the last page closes with a quotation from Abraham Lincoln stating "Our reliance is in the love of liberty which God has planted in us."

In addition to traditional theism, traditional capitalist economics are also presumed to be the American way. A pamphlet called Militant Liberty, authorized by Defense Secretary Charles Wilson, formerly a General Electric executive, and issued from the office of Admiral Radford in 1955, declares that "we, as free people ... believe in the true form and ideals of liberty."[34] It treats capitalism as the true American economic concept.[35] Equating capitalism with Americanism is characteristic of American Armed Forces ideology.[36]

In 1962, a carefully prepared ideological tract of 167 pages, approved by Secretary McNamara, was released to contrast American and Communist ideologies.[37] The thoughts of Adam Smith and other eighteenth and nineteenth century contributors to early American economic and political theory are used as examples of American ideology. No where are the massive changes in economic and political thought of this century revealed. A chapter on "Economic Order" quotes John Locke and his use of the theory of Natural Law in relation to "the right to own property." Remaining sections defend "Equality of economic opportunity, freedom of occupation and movement, the right to compete, and labor's right to organize and bargain," under a capitalistic conception of economics. The only type of economic planning that is described is communist totalitarian planning. The case is made for the economics of democratic capitalism, but democratic socialism is omitted as an ideology. Only two alternatives are described — captialism or communism.

The way the Armed Forces publications characterize American ideology is to utilize those traditional beliefs that are grounded in dogmatic preconceptions of human nature and society. The basis for such preference is not indicated. Though American society and American ideology are actually pluralistic, the Armed Forces ideology provides the distorted impression that the American way is monistic.

THE PARTISAN NATURE OF MILITARY IDEOLOGY

While there are many conflicts between the special Armed Forces brand of American ideology and the totalitarianism of military traditions, they do have some common elements. They are both absolutistic and are both offered as unequivocally right. They are both **pre-scientific** and therefore not treated as experimental hypotheses but as doctrines of inherent and self-evident truth. From the point of view of each of these ideologies, the only available choice is between that ideology and its single posed opposite. In other words, the narrowly defined alternatives offered are bi-polar instead of tri-polar or multi-polar, thus making the selection of an alternative a simplistic process.

In recent years the Americanism ideology held by the Armed Forces has been popularly labeled ''conservatism,'' while a rival public ideology is typically labeled ''liberalism.'' Conservatism, the more traditional view, considers man's nature to be predetermined so that social experience is at best only the opportunity for the individual to become what he was destined to become. All men are thought to have rights which are either divinely given or part of the laws of Nature. Protection of these rights is a primary reason for the existence of government. These rights, because of their connection with ultimate reality, are thought to be permanent and unchangeable. A man is free if he is freed from restrictions. Contemporary exponents of this ideology equate freedom largely as the freedom from government, for it is still remembered that the liberty of immigrant colonists had been restricted by European government, and the power of government is still strongly suspect to the conservative.

Economic theory under this ideology involves a natural ''law of supply and demand'' rather than government management of the distribution of goods and services. A natural balance is claimed to regulate prices and wages as individuals serve their self-interest competing with others.

This traditional view of market capitalism is opposed by those who endorse modern liberalism. The newer liberal conception of individualism emphasizes cooperation rather than competition including government's role in regulating and even controlling the economy. Environment is considered crucial to the development of human potentialities and so social-economic-political-educational planning is welcomed rather than feared, providing it results from the intelligent participation of those affected by the planning.

Though American political parties do not have very explicit ideologies the Democratic party usually emphasizes modern liberalism more than the Republican party. Ideological conflicts often underlie disputes between these two major political parties, and the 1964 presidential election made these differences especially clear, for Barry Goldwater, the Republican candidate made a special attempt to clarify the ideology of conservatism in his bid for power.

The Armed Forces, in their official Americanism ideology, appear to ignore the existence of any except the traditional position. A *partisan stand is taken* favoring what was called "conservatism" in the 1964 presidential election. The Armed Forces version of Americanism is one view of democratic theory, but it is only one kind of democratic theory. Modern Liberalism and democratic socialism are conspicuously omitted. Armed Forces Americanism assumes that the individual is pre-defined in a combination of supernatural-capitalistic terms, derived mainly from Christian idealism and pre-scientific, natural law realism. There is no statement in Armed Forces publications to admit that a selective process has taken place and that the Armed Forces have taken a partisan stand between democratic ideologies. Conservatism is offered as *the* American way, not as *an* American way. Theological sanction drawn from conservative views is used by the military to provide support for its selective ideology as well as absolute moral justification for American military involvement in the violence and killing connected with war.

In summary, it is seen that the American Armed Forces advance a simplistic ideology in which there is a "right" way and a "wrong" social philosophy in an absolute moral sense. The "right" way is the politics of conservative, capitalistic, traditional individualism. Freedom is therefore defined as lack of government involvement in a competitive economic system in which self-interest is the economic motive. This system is presumed to be based on a natural "law" of supply and demand. The more liberal conception of individualism is rejected, for it involves a cooperative rather than a competitive system, and it is based more on public planning and government management than merely a market system for the distribution of goods and services.

Though the United States has a mixture of both liberal and conservative ideologies and a mixture of practices, soldiers in the American Armed Forces are offered only a simple dichotomous conception of politics, which is, ironically, the same dichotomy used in communist propaganda. Communist ideology typically poses only alternatives between communism and capitalism, choosing the former. The American Armed Forces use the same "either-or" classification and choose the latter. Alternatives from both points of view are only between absolute good and absolute evil. The American soldier is taught that he is part of a country which is committed to a single point of view, and the American military teaches him what that view is to be.

IDEOLOGICAL JUSTIFICATION FOR A PARTICULAR WAR

Though "why we fight" materials were used extensively during World War II, it was after the Korean War that Armed Forces ideology emphasized "what we believe" to give justification for fighting. Many American soldiers held captive in Korea lacked defense against Communist persuasion. The high mortality rate of American prisoners during that period is well known. Although the accuracy of certain military reports has been seriously challenged, it continued to be a common, though apparently false belief that the high mortality rate resulted primarily from the ideological weakness of American soldiers. Since then the American military, particularly the Air Force, has focused on ideological defense. Post-Korean Armed Forces publications abound with statements on "why we fight" and "what we believe."

American soldiers are subjected, through pamphlets, films, radio, television, discussion, and lectures, to the military interpretation of Communism vs. Americanism. The "American" ideology is ordinarily labeled "free world" or "liberty."[38] It alone is set against communist ideology. A clear bi-polar dichotomy is offered. Soldiers are told:

Americans in Korea were up against it. They couldn't answer arguments in favor of communism with arguments in favor of Americanism . . . They needed to know such things as our capitalist economy is a constantly changing, flexible system. The wealth is constantly being spread on a broader base. Hundreds of thousands of steel workers, telephone operators and housewives are capitalists, owning shares of the nation's largest companies.[39]

America is on the side of God, Communism is atheistic — America stands for liberty; Communism stands for slavery — America means capitalism and therefore freedom; Communism means economic planning and therefore lack of freedom.

Communism is depicted as a monolithic world-wide conspiracy dedicated to a relentless battle against the values for which Americans live. *The Fighting Man's Code,* issued in 1959 as a response to Communist indoctrination in Korea, states: "International communism seeks world domination . . . All Communists are trained for one purpose — defeat of the capitalist democracies, especially the United States."[40]

An even more extreme statement is made in an Air Force publication titled *The Struggle for Men's Minds* (which includes *six pictures* of the Air Force ICBM).[41] It was published in 1960 for the stated purpose of influencing *public school counselors* to "help students maintain ability and will to fight." At the end of the pamphlet is a letter written "to the School Counselor" by a Lieutenant Colonel who says:

Today, as never before, an ideological struggle is on for men's minds on a universal scale with the total world population divided into two groups, democracy and communism. Because the communistic dictators insist that all other ways of life must ultimately give way to their own ideology, *there cannot be co-existence of democracy and communism, and the struggle is inevitably a mortal one.*

The God-America-Capitalism versus Atheism-UnAmerican-Communist point of view is so common in military documents that the alignment with the political right by most militarists is not surprising.

The most extreme case since World War II is General Edwin A. Walker's fanatical anti-communism which finally led to his dismissal when he tried to influence a presidential election. Other militarists found the Moral Re-armament program consistent with their theological foreign policy, without going quite as far to the right as Walker. Commitments to Moral Re-armament were made by militarists as private citizens, but Dr. Fred Schwarz's Christian Anti-Communist Crusade was officially embraced by at least one military training center, for his materials were distributed under the label of a naval base in San Diego.[42] Schwarz, an Australian physician, talked of communism as a disease and yet gave primarily theological and capitalistic reasons for opposing it. He advised that communism be taught "with a moral directive, in the same way that a medical student is taught that cancer is evil . . . If it is presented without moral direction, it appears simply as an alternative economic system with certain superior virtues. This has frequently been done in the past and instead of opposing communism, it tends to recruit to communism."[43]

Ideological "education" has been emphasized since the Korean War to tell American soldiers the "true" meaning of the American way of life. This process has continued during the Vietnam war, to give Americans within the Armed Forces the "correct" interpretation of both communism and Americanism. The pluralism of practices within many communist countries is obscured as is the variety of the practices within different communist countries. Similarly the Armed Forces omit the varieties of American ideology and the varieties of communist ideology. Instead, Armed Forces pamphlets offer an ideology closely connected to political conservatism, treating the Armed Forces as an incontestable authority on such matters. This orthodoxy is conveyed in various kinds of military pamphlets, especially those under the Armed Forces Information and Education program. They provide justifications for being in a particular war such as Vietnam in which the enemy can easily be labeled evil because he is "communist." When soldiers begin to question the simplistic presentations of ideology, they often begin to question the justification of U.S. presence in Vietnam as well.

WAR IDEOLOGY CLASSIFIED

Through polarizing conservatism and communism, the Armed Forces create two antithetical ideologies. Though the assumptions of communist ideology are sometimes subjected to scrutiny, conservatism is almost always taken on faith. Conservatism is assumed to represent the American way of life while communism is usually seen as a monolithic, irreconcilable force bent on world domination and the destruction of America.

Liberalism and fascism are conspicuously omitted as even theoretical ideological alternatives. When totalitarianism is occasionally used as a category it is associated only with communism, even though most of the totalitarian countries of the twentieth century have been fascistic rather than communistic.

Since the "free world" is defined as the non-communist world, it is implied that the U.S. is enjoying this kind of "freedom" along with the numerous fascistic military dictatorships. Strange classifications produce strange bedfellows.

CONCLUSIONS

American Armed Forces take the responsibility for trying to get American soldiers to have the "right" thoughts. Though the indoctrination process is not as intense as with soldiers in communist China, its function is similar. It consists of political indoctrination designed to get soldiers to accept prescribed beliefs. Information about values is narrowly selected to bring the soldier to the desired conclusion and therefore violates the standards of education acceptable in an open society.

For example, a text that has been widely used in college as an introduction to ideology makes two broad classifications — totalitarianism and democracy. But under totalitarianism both communism and fascism are described, and under democracy both democratic capitalism and democratic socialism are discussed. These are typical minimum ideological distinctions, offering four possibilities instead of only the two offered by the Armed Forces. Education requires an honest effort to reveal various points of view, keeping inquiry open, but Armed Forces troop indoctrination is designed to close inquiry and provide the official conclusion.

Political indoctrination is a questionable activity for any government agency within a democracy. When it is implemented within the military system it poses many serious problems. It means that the United States, which claims to have *goals* which are ideologically different from totalitarian countries, is, however, engaged in totalitarian *procedures*. The American soldier, often a draftee who is conscripted under penalty of law, is coerced to conform to military values. He is told that he is defending the values of his country, though many of the values he is asked to believe and to promote are selected by the Armed Forces. The Armed Forces version of Americanism encourages the soldier to hate and fight political systems that do not conform to American conservatism.

Distortion is not only a disservice to the individual soldier but to the nation as well. It contradicts our faith in an informed citizenry and offers blinders rather than clearer vision to the American soldier. For instance, a pamphlet series distributed by the Armed Forces Information and Education agency included a publication titled "The Truth About Our Economic System" which glowingly described American affluence but gave no indication of the existence of poverty in the United States. Yet at least one-fifth of the American population lives in poverty. The same series devoted an issue to communist countries and concentrated on *their poverty* problems. Another issue was devoted to "Soviet Treaty Violations," mentioning nothing about Soviet treaties which were not violated nor anything about American violations of international law.[44] America's treaty violations, from the American Indian on, makes quite a list itself.

American Armed Forces ideological indoctrination raises serious questions for the larger society. If our society is to remain democratic, political indoctrination should be removed from military training. Legitimate education does not pre-determine the "right" conclusions and therefore must not be controlled by the military, the Department of Defense, or the State Department. All these agencies have interests which conflict with open educational objectives. Open education would produce a defensible basis for morale and probably increase willingness of soldiers to fight in those situations where it made sense, while morale might sag when objectives were questionable.

An open society protects itself from providing foolish and fanatical support of unwise objectives. Armed Forces indoctrination may be one reason why American troops in Vietnam have been more convinced about the justification of the war than civilians who have somewhat less confining sources of information.

It is dangerous for a country to use deception while claiming to serve the goals of democracy. It undermines open-democratic values and distorts the actual reasons why men are conscripted to fight and die. Even more, the kind of political indoctrination used in the Armed Forces probably increases the likelihood of World War III by manipulating the awareness of the trainee and by limiting and distorting the ideological alternatives. To the extent that those distortions begin to pervade our society, we make war more likely by subverting our own political intelligence.

CHAPTER III

CREATING MARINES:
MILITARISM PAR EXCELLENCE

Although the Marine Corps is only one of five branches of the Armed Forces, it may be worth giving special attention to the Marines and their values. They are often labeled as an elite military corps. Whereas other branches, especially the Air Force, make much use of technology and individual specialization to achieve their strength, the Marines rely on creating a tough member of a corps, capable of the best close combat fighting the military has to offer.

The Marines spend a good deal of effort in self-glorification, but they are no different from the other military branches in this respect. They have become, however, more successful in creating a popular image of tough invincibility, a sort of mayhem mystique. They are, perhaps, the closest thing America has to compare with the famed German SS.

When the President requires a special force, either to make a landing and rout a revolution as in the Dominican Republic, or to cope with recalcitrant revolutionaries in Vietnam — the Marines are called out. Whether or not it is in fact justified, the announcement is usually made with the assurance that somehow we are now all saved.

The Marines expect the recruit to fit into the Corps and to develop a life long ''Marine'' personality. They do not characterize the Marines as semi-civilian, rather they set their corps off as highly military and distinctive — militarism par excellence. They have special traditions and special functions that guide their general military commitment. They must be ready for duty ashore and also on the sea, as an assault corps and as an arm of the Navy to secure advanced bases. Their training, however, involves a problem shared by all branches of the military, namely that there is no sound experimental evidence that the particular traditions which retain such a strong hold on military training and on the military way of life are really necessary to accomplish their mission. It is tenaciously assumed, by members of these subcultures, that their particular training is necessary. But until there is more evidence, all we can scientifically conclude is that ''that is the way it is done,'' but not that ''that is the way it must be done.''

Lack of any serious criticism of Marine training indicates that both the Marines and the supporting civilian establishment *assume* that such a way of life is absolutely justified. Therefore, the recruit's induction into this way of life is allowed by our government to be both rapid and total. Marine training makes maximum use of the concept of shock treatment and traumatic conversion. In many ways it resembles the puberty rites of the pre-literate societies, where transition from childhood to adulthood is made abruptly and dramatically. Marines appear to favor this particular analogy, because they constantly refer to the process as "turning boys into men." What they actually turn them into needs to be examined.

The traditions of Marine Corps training were given a public airing in 1956 when the well-publicized Parris Island incident occurred. A drill sergeant took fresh recruits in a non-authorized night march to teach them some "discipline." Aided by a few drinks of vodka, he led them into brackish waters up to seven feet deep and told them that "anyone who can't swim is going to drown. Those who can swim will be eaten by the sharks!"[1] There was panic and before long six had drowned in Ribbon Creek. The publicity and subsequent inquiries revealed the standards of brutality which had been normal practice in the Marine Corps training.

The American Civil Liberties Union sent questionnaires to ex-Marines after the Parris Island incident. The "overwhelming majority" said that maltreatment by Marine Corps drill instructors was a daily sight at Parris Island. Ninety-four percent had seen recruits slapped by drill instructors. Eighty-four percent had seen recruits struck with the fist by drill instructors, 85 percent had seen recruits kicked, and 84 percent had seen them struck with swagger sticks.[2]

Nearly all the public responses to the brutality were critical of the Marines. There were two notable exceptions, George Lincoln Rockwell and General "Chesty" Puller. Rockwell, then head of the American Nazi Party, wrote in the *American Mercury* that he strongly identified with the Marines though he had only been attached to them for a while in World War II. He said he knew they used "tough, dangerous training . . . the last stronghold of the tough, aristocratic, iron disciplined tradition." To be a Marine is to "fight" he said, and "you can't learn to kill just by reading books." He urged that people "try trusting the Generals and the Admirals for a change."[3]

The general who had been "trusted" and who was then Commandant of the Marine Corps did not think that McKeon, the drill sergeant at Parris Island, should have been "ordered to trial by general court martial."[4] He apparently did not consider McKeon's behavior to be a serious violation of Marine Corps standards.

Another trusted general was "Chesty" Puller, hero of the Marine Corps and previous commander of Marine basic training in San Diego. He testified that there was nothing wrong with the practices of the drill instructor in the Parris Island incident, in fact, it was "good military tactics."[5] He stated that he had always given drill instructors "practically unlimited authority" and he testified that it had been his practice "to train troops as he thought they should be trained, regardless of directives." He seemed to condone any practice which was thought to produce "success in battle," and he added that "the two prime requisites of a Marine are perfect physical condition and immediate and automatic acceptance of orders."

The heroes of one institution may be very different from the heroes of another, depending on the values of each institution. A biography of General Puller offers some suggestions of the values which made him so successful in the Marines.[6] Though Puller's biographer tries to be eulogistic, the General comes through as a man who believed in "my country, right or wrong," and who not only fought and killed for his country but *enjoyed* doing it. He had devoted his life to fighting and killing and had even hired out as a mercenary before he became famous in World War II, earning the name of Il Tigre in the banana wars and allegedly paying bounty for the ears of native bandits. He fought through many of the bloodiest battles of World War II and came out of retirement to fight in Korea. Convinced of the invincibility of both himself and the Marines, he dedicated himself so thoroughly to victory that when new American reinforcements dug in near the enemy, its colonel asked where their line of retreat would be. Puller answered by calling his tank commander and ordering him to open fire on our *own* troops "if they start to pull back from that line, even one foot."[7] Casualities from his own troops were high, but the Communist losses were much higher. After the war he retired, laden with decorations, and he is now a military legend.

His postwar interests include trying to build a Marine Corps for his close friend, Chiang Kai-shek. In advising Chiang on the strategy of a mainland invasion, Puller's biographer says he told Chiang that "Most important of all . . . he must put to death every Communist bastard he meets. There can be no quarter." He was apparently not called on again for moral, political, or military advice until the Parris Island incident.

The biographer tells of the General's exceptional pleasure when his eleven year old boy killed a deer. Apparently the General detected unusual promise through such an achievement. After his permanent retirement his wife asked him what he now wished for and he replied, "I'd like to do it all over again. The whole thing."

General Puller belonged to an era in Marine Corps history when overt, brutal coercion was normal in Marine training. McKeon's trial and the related hearings forced the Corps into some modification of its methods, particularly when one more grotesque incident soon became news involving mistreatment by Marines in the Naval brig at Sasebo, Kyushu, Japan. One writer, typical of the critics, said:

> The dozen or so Marines convicted of maltreating prisoners did not indulge in such practices without having precedent for them. Somewhere in their military careers they were given to understand that almost any method was justified in the name of producing a "tough" fighting man or, presumably, in the name of reforming prisoners. Somewhere their immediate supervisors had gotten the same idea . . . They are as much the victims of misguided training policy as were the six trainees who died in the ill-fated night march.[8]

44

By 1959, three years after the Parris Island hearings, a *New York Times* reporter visited Parris Island and found that the commander had repressed practices "offending against human dignity." Whereas previous training had utilized "sadism and brutality," drill instructors were by 1959 ordered not to produce "any fracture, concussion, contusion, or welt." A whole list of honored traditions were officially banned including:

1. Hazing.
2. Causing recruits to run unnecessarily up and down ladders or in and out of buildings.
3. Causing recruits to ingest more food or beverage than their normal consumption.
4. Causing recruits to ingest any paper or other foreign matter not commonly used as food for human consumption.
5. Causing recruits to march or drill with ballast in pockets or pack.
6. Causing recruits to participate in an assault against each other.
7. Causing recruits to inflict unnecessary pain upon themselves, to collide unnecessarily with physical objects such as causing them to run into a wall.
8. Causing recruits to stand in unnatural positions for undue lengths of time such as doing "wall bends."[9]

The reporter said the drill instructors now talked more like psychiatrists and concentrated on psychological manipulation rather than the former physical coercion. Some were disappointed in the reforms but "a crowd of sergeants at the drill instructors school insisted they could mold the recruits by 'persuasive leadership.'"

The article reported the post General as saying, "The basic philosophy of Marine training hasn't changed much. We take kids who don't have the slightest conception of discipline and make them into guys you can take to war."

It is by no means possible to turn off traditions suddenly through official pronouncement, but since 1959 physical brutality has not been *officially* authorized and the recruit now has *some* recourse against unofficial physical brutality, provided he is still alive. Ten years later, in 1969 another recruit died of injuries received in training at Parris Island![10] Sadistic drill instructors were usually careful to avoid lethal injuries, but they still managed, as one recruit said, "to beat the hell out of him everyday."[11] And in 1969 reports from Camp Pendleton were confirmed that prisoners were brutalized.[12]

Marine Corps goals continue to be essentially the same, and the Corps is permeated with many of the old attitudes, but officially authorized coercion and manipulation must now be primarily psychological. This process is revealed in an interesting public relations film made at the Marine Crops Recruit Depot in San Diego since the official termination of training brutality. The film is treated as a documentary and was produced by a commercial company, but it consists of a carefully planned film showing 11 weeks of Marine training with actual recruits, presented in such a manner as to exemplify Marine training at its *best*. It is worth examining the action and the dialogue to identify the values that are stressed even under these exemplary conditions.

The recruits are first shown marching into the base with the noticeable individuality of different styles of civilian clothes and haircuts. The stern and pugnacious drill sergeant singles out one of the recruits and harshly admonishes him to ''look straight in the front . . . keep your eyes there all the time. Is that clear?''

Soon the commentator explains what is occurring and says:

''Youngsters who enlist in the Marine Corps are joining an elite group of fighting men, one of the most lethal combat teams in the world. Such men are not born, they are made in 11 weeks of remarkable training. To the average civilian, perhaps, this training may seem too tough, too grueling. The drill instructors may appear harsh and callous, but every hour, every day of Marine training is carefully designed to take youngsters out of un-disciplined civilian life and turn them into crack fighting men. This training works and in the end those who go through it look back on it with a special pride . . . the boy who finally graduates from boot camp is a Marine.''

Next we see the ''men'' (actually boys) in the barracks and they are now told by the sergeant:

'' . . . Suck your stomach in and raise your chest up, hold your head erect. Pick out an imaginary spot directly in front of you and stare at it. You don't look up and down or side to side. All you do is stand there and breathe. Any time that it becomes necessary for you to speak, the first word out of your mouth at all times will be Sir. Sir, my name is Private Smith. Sir, I am 17 years old— whichever the case may be. You don't smoke, chew gum, eat candy . . . *you don't do anything unless you are told to.* Anytime that someone tells you to do something, you do it as fast as humanly possible — that is as fast as you can possibly move. (etc.)''

The announcer then explains:

''The first premise of Marine training is to *take away every trace of a recruit's former life,* then *remold him* into a Marine. To begin with, the recruits must *all look* the same. This is where the civilian starts to disappear.''13

The viewer then sees the recruits led into the barber shop, later to emerge with crew cuts, all looking very much (as the announcer has said) ''the same.'' When they get into identical uniforms the metamorphosis of appearance does become remarkable. The announcer confirms, ''Now the last traces of civilian life are taken away.'' The sergeant then explains procedures, stating menacingly, ''you will do exactly as we tell you. You will not ask who, what, when, where, or why.''

While the recruits obtain supplies in a highly regimented way, the sergeant singles out ''individuals'' who are having difficulty and badgers them into saying they have no excuse for any of their problems and that they want to conform and to become a Marine.

The Sergeant yells orders at separate recruits and at squadrons and demands immediate response. He wants only a ''Yes Sir'' or ''No Sir'' reply to direct questions. He later explains to the viewer, ''This is the way you turn boys into fighting men. You have to teach them how to function under constant pressure. On the battlefield there is no room for delicate feelings . . . '' Soon the recruits are shown in training. They stand in two lines across from each other, and at the signal they rush out with ''pugil sticks,'' which have a heavy knob of material on each end of a strong stick. The job is to beat the other fellow with your stick more than he can beat you. The process is similar to fighting with a rifle butt, though it is obvious that the training is concerned with more than mere techniques. The narrator explains:

''The first time they come rushing out, their mind is completely blank because they're so scared. You know some of these boys have never been in a fight before, but the next time they're vibrating and they just can't wait until they can get in there again. I think it is a turning point for many of them . . . ''

Much of the remaining film shows the sergeant continually harassing individual Marines by such means as singling out a recruit and yelling degrading and humiliating remarks while they are forced to stand at attention and obediently respond with ''Yes Sir'' or ''No Sir.'' Finally the Sergeant ruminates: ''Physically they are nothing, mentally pretty good, but *you got to break them down, break them all the way down* and then gradually, gradually up . . . ''

At the end of the training the narrator concludes, over the background music of ''The Halls of Montezuma'':

''Men have been molded into a compact efficient group capable of obeying commands with precision and with pride. Tomorrow (they) will graduate . . . (then they will be) Marines, and they will be Marines not only as long as they are in the Corps but for the rest of their lives.''

The psychology underlying this kind of training is loaded with totalitarian assumptions. The first goal is to get rid of individuality, to create uniformity and loss of previous identity. The new identity is the identity of the corps, and the corps is defined through the instructional elite. The training officers are transmitters of the values of the organization. Through punishment and reward, repetition, and the relentless imposition of new patterns, they get the recruit to acquire a Marine identity. Embarrassment and humiliation psychologically destroy the recruit, leaving him broken and defenseless, or cause him to develop an inner hostility which can be channeled into combat hostility. Once the rough, aggressive, obedient Marine is developed, he has achieved totalitarian ''freedom.'' He has lost individual identity and is now ''free'' only to do what he is told to do. He is no longer an individual, he is now a Marine.

This tight indoctrination process often works with remarkable efficiency, but like all teaching systems it is not perfect. All members of the Marine Corps are not blind and fanatically obedient. One perceptive Marine Sergeant of twenty years experience (who asked that he not be identified) was highly objective in describing the corps. He pointed out for this study some of the following characteristics of the Marines as he has observed them during the last 20 years.

Marine recruits volunteer in the sense that they have selected the Marines instead of another branch of the military. This self-selection tends to produce somewhat of a type. ''Marines seem to possess a pugnaciousness that in some cases borders upon pathology,'' he said. ''In combat, this may be well and good, but it's tough on day-to-day relationships.'' The Marine Corps, according to the Sergeant, ''attracts tough, adventuresome, pugnacious, aggressive youth who see in the Corps a place to prove themselves or vent their aggressive energies respectfully in an organization which boasts of its man-making qualifications. They seem to equate these qualities with genuine manliness.'' The Sergeant denies that most recruits join primarily for patriotic reasons.

The Sergeant adds that the Marines make little use of explicit ideology, as is used in the Air Force. They ''know little about Communism or any other ideology including our own.'' They are given ''little indoctrination in the so-called 'why we fight'sense.'' They are trained ''to obey orders and it is my unwavering belief that in the main they have always and will always obey. Those who can't or won't obey just don't last in the Marine Corps.'' The Marines are not just obedient in their willingness to attack the enemy, but if they were told to they would ''cheerfully fight the U.S. Army, U.S. Navy, or U.S. Air Force.''

The Sergeant was asked: ''Does there seem to be any awareness on the part of the Marines that killing is their business and that there is a sense in which they are voluntary murderers?'' He stated:

''Basically the DI (Drill Instructor) indoctrinates the Marine recruit with an ultimately simplified, kill philosophy. You kill that other bastard before he kills you. There is no great ideological question involved here, not even in the Fascistic sense. Pure Darwinian, I would suggest. Marines normally mince no words about being in the killing business. They are taught the business that way. The typical Marine drill instructor will say with feeling, We are not here to teach you to die for your country, we are here to teach you how to help some other son of a bitch die for his

48

country. With this attitude firmly inculcated, the question of voluntary murder becomes academic.

"The central goal of current training is," as General Wallace M. Greene said recently, To kill Cong! He might have added — or anyone else that Marines have been directed to attack. Never point the gun unless you mean to pull the trigger, is a Marine adage. When you pull the trigger, be sure you have aimed the weapon at a vital area."[14]

The Sergeant's direct experience with the Marines stands slightly in contrast to a Marine recruiting poster which uses a pacifistic and innocent looking Marine, nattily dressed, standing by an equally pink-cheeked female Marine. They are shown standing in a church, looking piously upward. The poster is titled, "Always Faithful."

The cherubic piety of recruiting-poster Marines seems to have minimum effect on actual Marine behavior. Though the Marines try to enforce the Uniform Code of Military Justice as much as the other branches of the Armed Forces, the Marine crime rate is especially high. The problem may be that by attracting and creating a tough, belligerent type of soldier and by enforcing a stern, totalitarian environment, they get the behavioral results that would be expected, according to the findings of studies of autocratic and authoritarian environments. Such studies consistently show a high level of hostility and aggressiveness in a tightly disciplined environment, a finding that contradicts those who hold that tight external discipline leads to greater self-discipline. For instance, in 1964[15] the record of military crimes in Hawaii which were brought to trial through court-martial revealed that the "well disciplined" Marines were involved in 19 times more courts martial than the less disciplined members of the Air Corps. And the Marines were given company punishment over *seven* times as often as the Air Force personnel. This differential is impressive when it is seen that this crime *rate* is not affected by differences in total numbers of men. Furthermore, both the Air Force and the Marines had such a sizable number of men in Hawaii that this comparison for an entire year is significant.

It is a fact highly verified by penologists and psychologists that an environment stressing harsh totalitarian control usually produces not the most pacifistic members of society but rather the most dangerous and aggressive members. It seems that when a human being is treated like putty, to be molded according to external demands, as is attempted by the Marine Corps, there are likely to be many individually and socially destructive side effects. Bruno Bettelheim has contributed much to our understanding of the psychological problems and effects of a totalitarian environment. Psychologist Bettelheim survived the experience of Nazi concentration camps and has written the famous study of totalitarianism and human identity, "The Informed Heart." His findings have bearing on an evaluation of the military values of the American Marine Corps.

UNINFORMED HEARTLESSNESS

"I had to accept that the environment could, as it were, turn personality upside down, and not just in the small child, but in the mature adult too," Bettelheim states.[16] Psychoanalysis is not the most effective way to change personality; rather, "being placed in a particular type of environment can produce much more radical changes and in a much shorter time."[17]

Bettelheim does not claim that everyone responds identically to a particular environmental influence. Some hold on to values internalized early in life, some develop interplay which produces a new personality integration, while others permit the new environment to take over entirely. But when totalitarian influences are highly organized there are few people who can escape destruction of whatever autonomy they had developed. The devices of effective totalitarian conversion must take account of a number of psychological considerations, each aimed at depersonalization. Numbers, ranks and grades are often substituted for individualizing names. Interpersonal contact and especially love relationships must be denied or at least minimized. The Nazi system, as it culminated in the treatment of concentration camp prisoners, became the apotheosis of totalitarian control. It denied privacy, took away individual responsibility, created the appearance of uniformity through identical dress, and made the salute mandatory. "The Nazi system was built on the leader principle; the rank and file had simply to obey without questioning."[18] Those who "showed any hesitation about falling in line had to be forced by intimidation."[19]

As people are stripped of their identity, says Bettelheim, they look to something else to provide it. The more absolute the tyranny, the more it is necessary to gain some kind of strength by becoming part of the tyranny and enjoying its power.[20] A tyranny that makes ruthless use of power therefore can create not merely enemies but also many converts to *serve* the system, if it has utilized methods which are effective in destroying individual identity and offers a new identity within the system. Or if a person has little sense of identity to begin with, there can be a largely voluntary attachment to a tyrannical system. Individual responsibility is then replaced by unquestioning obedience.

Bettelheim's description of the psychology of fascism is essentially the same as Erich Fromm's. Studying the psychological basis for Western man's "escape from freedom" into a tyrannical mass state, Fromm concludes that "the insignificance and powerlessness of the individual"[21] are fertile soil for fascism. "The more the drive toward life is thwarted, the stronger is the drive toward destruction; the more life is realized, the less is the strength of destructiveness." Other students of psychology and mass behavior come to essentially the same conclusion. Loss of personal identity and the creation of self-hatred tend to strengthen one's attachment to a strong and ruthless system, providing a need for a vicarious sense of identity and aggressive power.

50

The "psychology of fascism," especially as it is described by Bettelheim through his exierence with Nazism, provides striking parallels with the training psychology of the American Marines. They, too, eliminate individual identity as rapidly and as traumatically as possible, by regimentation, by uniformity of appearance through clothing and haircuts, by identification with the military through an anonymous serial number and rank, by putting trainees in a "goldfish bowl" barracks without privacy and without personal possessions which express individuality. Deviation from orders results in rapid and traumatic humiliation, and the recruit is taught that virtually all external behavior, even facial expression and the direction of the eyes, must conform to the demands of the drill sergeant. There is the continuous promise that conversion will be rewarded with real manhood and that what one is leaving behind is only immaturity.

The period of basic training carefully excludes the Marine from his previous environment, much as the monastery excludes the outside world. The recruit is kept busy from morning until night, so that he has little time for contemplation, reflection, or conversation. He often concentrates on sheer physical survival. Each day he conforms, it becomes easier and more imperative that he do so the following day. At first he may hate his sadistic "superiors." But if the process is successful, and it usually is, he begins to identify with them. As his own identity disappears, he models himself after his own tormentors, and he is soon ready to carry aggression and hostility to who ever is called an "enemy." And he is ready to demand of other Marines the same uncompromising obedience and devotion to "duty."

Insofar as he has become a Marine, he has lost his old identity, weak as that may have been, and has taken the goals of the corps as his own. What has happened is psychologically comparable to the creation of the devout Nazi, yet it is done in the name of protecting American democracy, as though the ends of democracy could be separated from the means of sustaining it. It is significant that of the various branches of the American military, the Marines are the least interested in ideology. They need no explicit ideology, for the commitment to both violence and obedience provides an implicit ideology and a non-verbal sense of totalitarian identity.

In 1965, the President changed the self-selection tradition of the Marines by ordering draftees into the Corps. There has been little public recognition of the human price being asked of these draftees nor much concern whether a state (particularly one which professes democratic values) has any right to ask its young men to pay such a price. It is one thing to defend one's country but quite another to have that country control the very meaning of one's life by imposing the values and the procedures supposedly reserved only to the morally depraved "enemy."

The other branches of the service also make use of many of the fascist totalitarian values of the Marines. In the cold and hot war of the last two and a half decades, military values have been increasingly accepted as a normal part of the general American value system, often in the sincere belief that militarism is vital to the cause of freedom. It is typically assumed that civilian "free" America is the end which justifies military means, and it is also assumed that the means and the ends can be held in separation. This is the tragic fallacy of our age — the failure to see that the means largely determine the ends. Military establishments in American society serve as both means and ends, though this is often denied in popular mythology.

The military outlook is not only interwoven in a huge system of military-industrial power, but is also a normal part of the civilian outlook, determining many of our political goals. Increasingly, when we believe we need the military to solve an international problem, we overlook the possibility that we may have made the use of violence into the only perceived solution.

PART II

TEACHING FOR WAR THROUGH
CIVILIAN INSTITUTIONS

CHAPTER IV

TEACHING MILITARY VALUES
WITHIN AMERICAN SOCIETY

A. THE MILITARY METAPHYSIC

The central belief in a military metaphysic is that threat systems based on organized violence are the foundation for international order. This outlook developed long before the existence of the nation-state, but it is expressed in the modern world in conjunction with the nation-state system. The military metaphysic is seldom merely an isolated belief, more often it is part of a larger outlook encompassing assumptions about human nature. The outlook is widely shared by both civilians and militarists within the United States, and a retired politician is as likely as a retired general to write a book supportive of the outlook.

A retired Commander-in-Chief of the Strategic Air Command of the United States, General Thomas Power, wrote a book which provided a clear statement of the military metaphysic. Quotations will be taken from General Power's book followed by the principle of the military metaphysic that is implied. The General states:

(1) "The price we would have to pay for survival through disarmament and eventual world-government would be gradual surrender of our national sovereignty. This is a price which I consider far higher than the price we are paying for survival through deterence and, in fact, a price which is utterly unacceptable to me."[1]

The principle implied here is that THE ONLY WORLD WORTH HAVING IS ONE ORGANIZED THROUGH NATION-STATES. The General assumes that one should gain his identification and the meaning of this life only through his connection to a nation, for a world based on international control would deprive life of significant meaning. On the question of international conflict he says:

(2) "For how long do we have to keep up a credible military deterrent? For as long as our survival is threatened; that is, indefinitely."[2]

A second principle is implied, that CONFLICT IS INEVITABLE BETWEEN NATIONS. No suggestion is offered for developing a more cooperative international system. The established political organization is assumed to be the only way in which men ought to live. No improved system of conflict management is proposed.

(3) "The basic reason for having a military is to do two jobs—to kill people and to destroy the works of man . . . . I am confident that the majority of the American people will . . . continue to support

our national policy of deterrence as the only acceptable solution to the problem of *national* survival."[3]

The third principle of the military metaphysic as articulated by Power is that NATIONAL CONFLICT SHOULD BE CONTROLLED BY THE THREAT OF A NATIONAL MILITARY FORCE. Presumably people are non-rational and controllable only by punishment. Only a threat to people's lives will secure the social order.

His logic guarantees that military deterrence will always be necessary, for the other nation is always to be distrusted. With no mention of America's failures at keeping treaties, General Power makes the often-stated assertion that:

(4) "Any pacts and agreements with the Soviets can be expected to be as meaningless and one-sided in the future as they have been in the past."[4]

This fourth principle is that AN ENEMY IS MORALLY DEPRAVED AND MACHIAVELLIAN, THEREFORE INCAPABLE OF ESTABLISHING RELIABLE AGREEMENTS. Presumably human beings do not behave according to a common set of social-psychological principles but rather according to a fixed moral condition that favors "our" side. Our nation is morally superior and their nation is morally inferior, therefore they can never be trusted, only contained. This depravity is explained by the general:

(5) "The Soviet leadership is irrevocably committed to the achievement of the ultimate Communist objective, which is annilation of the capitalist system and establishment of Communist dictatorship over all nations of the world."[5]

The fifth principle implied in this statement, is that NATIONS DIVIDE THEMSELVES INTO IRRECONCILABLE IDEOLOGICAL CAMPS WITH THEIR SIDE WANTING TO OVERTHROW OUR WAY OF LIFE. This assumes that the "other" side will do anything to achieve its goals, so that the world at its best can consist only of a cold war. The way to avoid a hot war is said to be to prepare for one.

(6) "The first and in my opinion, foremost principle is to maintain a *credible* capacity to achieve a military victory under any set of conditions and circumstances. The second basic principle is to make certain that the Soviets and any other potential aggressors *know* at all times that we have that capacity."[6]

The sixth principle is that TO HAVE THE CAPACITY TO ANNIHILATE AND THE WILLINGNESS TO DO IT IS THE ONLY WAY TO DETER AGGRESSION. This deterrence theory assumes that the enemy militarizes for aggression while we militarize only for peace. This ethnocentrism pervades the military metaphysic. The world is seen from the point of view only of one's own nation. Since technology is the source of military power, General Power logically concludes:

(7) "It would be folly to assume that nuclear weapons are the

ultimate in firepower and that nuclear missiles are the ultimate weapon. In the years ahead, the ever accelerating pace of scientific advancement is bound to reach new plateaus of military technology which will make today's most advanced weapons seem crude and ineffective . . . . All this is a frightful prospect to contemplate but we must be realistic and face the facts, however unpleasant.''[7]

The seventh and last principle is that TECHNOLOGICAL ADVANCES WILL PERPETUALLY EXPAND THE ARMS RACE, YET THIS IS THE ONLY ACCEPTABLE COURSE OF ACTION. We see that there is to be no cessation in the construction of armament. Overkill is not enough; we must perfect the speed and the strategy by which we can more than annihilate; we must escalate overkill. Freedom and national defense require unchanging *goals,* so the only problems which can be solved are those relating to the scientific and technical *means.* Deterrence requires the perpetual escalation of terror.

These are the elements of the military metaphysic in its modern context. They are grounded in an acceptance of self-interest, evil, in-group out-group morality, and a strong faith in technology. The assumptions reflect many of the cultural beliefs held by Americans. Yet a world dominated by the military metaphysician's threat of violence rather than law and cooperation is as dangerous as a nation run by rival bands of armed vigilantes. If the vigilantes from each clan have control of atomic weapons as have modern nations, and if they proclaim that it is ''power for peace'' as does our Department of Defense, it can easily become power for suicide. Instead of it being a ''design for survival'' as General Power contends, this outlook is the design for World War III.

Note that the General assumes (in his last quote) that he has been ''facing the facts,'' whereas he has been selecting those facts that conform to his conclusions. If he faced some of the new facts connected with survival in the atomic age, he may have difficulty holding a military metaphysic. He justifies his position on the basis of its being ''realistic'' without recognizing that the position itself has defined reality. The military metaphysic is self-contained political fundamentalism. With consistent myopia the General reasons that we must continue ''progress'' toward the truly ultimate weapon.

But the militarist outlook is not limited to the professional soldier. It has been endemic in most *civilian* policy. American life was transformed by World War II and has never recovered, for that was when the military-industrial complex was born. In an unplanned society it constituted a new form of planning which provided jobs and profits after the grim decade of the 1930s.

After the war, Russia was abandoned as an ally and anti-communism once again pre-occupied, sometimes obsessed American political thought, and the cold war was born. Military expenditure kept the economy in motion and anti-communism provided national purpose.

Civilian presidents and their civilian advisors (with Pentagon assistance) produced a foreign policy based on fear of the military expansion of communist countries. The political and economic injustices underlying indigenous revolution has never been accepted as a central reason for political change. So America became the keeper of the status quo—either through military power or through arms and economic support provided often to unrepresentative national governments. Suppression of insurgent movements in other countries has been a major goal of American foreign policy.

This policy has often required direct American intervention such as in Greece (1944), Iran (1953), Guatemala (1954), Lebanon (1958), Cuba (1961), Dominican Republic (1965), Cambodia (1970), Laos (1971) and the well known case where intervention since 1954 produced a few problems—Vietnam.[8] The support of "desirable" governments and the subversion of "undesirable" governments has required the active cooperation of the Pentagon, the C.I.A., and the State Department. Foreign aid programs have been used as a "carrot" to serve these same anti-communist objectives.

No civilian figure has been more influential than John Foster Dulles in supporting a military metaphysic. He proclaimed that "communist control of any government anywhere is in itself a danger and a threat."[9] He considered communists to be godless and therefore Anti-American, but he found no such difficulties with fascist military governments. At first he was an influential advisor in the State Department, later he was Secretary of State under Eisenhower where he shaped the nuclear deterrence policy, helped plan the policy of military containment of communist countries, and he encouraged Eisenhower to saturate the "free world" with military bases and introduced the policy of nuclear brinkmanship.

It takes at least two powers to have an arms race, and so both the United States and Russia must accept their share of responsibility for arms escalation. But the United States has insisted on superiority. There was some logic to a policy of arms superiority when military strength had some possible relationship to national *defense*. But this point was past long ago. The Russians are now as vulnerable to our ICBMs as we are to theirs. This is now the era of "overkill" when we continue obsessively to build a military force which will *more than annihilate*. The dim realization that military escalation has brought new heights of *national insecurity* has led us to even *more* reliance on military "solutions." The Vietnam war was escalated again and again to bring about "peace" in Asia, reminiscent of George Santayana's point that a fanatic is one who intensifies his effort once he has lost his aims.

Criminals who serve many years in confinement will often, upon release, begin to steal or to do whatever caused the incarceration and punishment in the first place. This behavior seems absurd from an outside point of view. Why take risks that may lead to the same dire consequences?

The problem is that a particular outlook may have been the only one the man had developed. He may perceive of life only as a process of stealing and trying to escape.

The analogy seems applicable to many of those who see the world through the military metaphysic. They may decide that the ''solution'' to a problem is ''to send in the Marines.'' If the Marines don't solve it, send in the Army—then the Air Corps. Begin with light bombing. If this doesn't solve it, try heavy bombing. If this doesn't solve it—expand the effort again and again. Such a course of action, of course, cannot go on indefinitely. Its inner logic does force an eventual ''showdown.'' While the persistent thief eventually goes back to jail, the modern nation that persists in winning ''peace'' through escalation of violence is likely to go back to the Stone Age. The thief may decide that his seemingly unavoidable jail is bad but tolerable. The military metaphysician seems to have been swayed by the same psychology. For him World War III becomes undesirable but tolerable.

Herman Kahn in his well-known book *On Thermonuclear War* offered elaborate theory to predict the time it would take the United States (the nation, not the individual citizens) to recover from nuclear attack. If only 20,000,000 were killed, he estimated, ''recovery'' could occur in 10 years. However, if 160,000,000 were killed it would take approximately 100 years. Those who hold to the deterrence theory must be willing to accept such mass death in any case where deterrence fails to deter.

To one who views the world outside the military metaphysic, international conflict resolution based on a threat of annihilation is a world out of control headed toward unnecessary disaster. Jerome Wiesner and Herbert F. York contend that:

''Both sides in the arms race are thus confronted by the dilemma of steadily increasing military power and steadily decreasing national security. *It is our considered professional judgment that this dilemma has no technical solution. If the great powers continue to look for solutions in the area of science and technology only, the result will be to worsen the situation. The clearly predictable course of the arms race is a steady open spiral downward into oblivion.* ''[10]

Harrison Brown and James Real estimate that a 10-megaton warhead, half the size our B-52 bombers can carry, dropped on central Los Angeles would create destruction not only by blast but particularly by a fire storm within a radius of at least 25 miles from the center of the blast. Only those in very deep shelters with built-in oxygen supplies would have any chance of surviving, and they would need to stay under for weeks.

Brown and Real point out that in 1959 a Special Subcommittee on Radiation (of the Joint Congressional Committee on Atomic Energy) estimated the following results of a 1500-megaton attack on the United States; Fifty million people would be expected to die, and 20,000,000 would be injured. Most industrial centers and the communication systems would be devastated, and sources of food and water would be largely radioactive and unusable. Yet nuclear escalation continues and the problems of the world continue to be analyzed by many leading newsmen, politicians, and prominent citizens through an essentially military outlook.

It is not clear whether our military metaphysic is so compulsively ingrained that it will persist in spite of the madness that it portends, or whether the consequences of the current outlook are not really understood. If it is the latter, there is still some basis for hope if leaders will search for human solutions with the same fervor now put into the search for a military "solution."[11]

B. THE SELF-FULFILLING PROPHECY

A genuine prophecy, such as those made in physical science, puts the prophet outside the process, predicting the course of natural events. A self-fulfilling prophecy is one in which the prophecy presumes to predict the future while it actually guides change in the direction of the prophecy.

Culture is a type of self-fulfilling prophecy. The assumptions about human nature, for instance, vary in each culture, but people in a particular culture expect others to conform to a pattern of behavior and hold the same expectations for themselves. It is hardly surprising that their prophecies about "human nature" usually turn out to be substantially accurate—people become "naturally" self-centered, cooperative, aggressive, lazy or whatever are the traits that are emphasized by that culture.[12]

The self-fulfilling prophecy is not merely applicable to so-called primitive societies, it is operative in modern America. Politicians make good use of it with such pronouncements as: "Americans are learning to distrust the other party" or "Patriotic Americans are supporting the President's policies in Vietnam." The statement is offered as a fact, but *in so far as it is believed* it becomes an instrument effecting the results that were forecast.

The military metaphysic, for example, not only describes a particular kind of reality—it becomes an instrument for creating it. As Professor Berman of the Harvard Law School pointed out, "American readers . . . often simply reject, subconsciously, those images which conflict with their preconceptions."[13]

The great irony of what we ordinarily call human freedom is that the *basis* for choice is the one thing a person is *least* likely to know. Values are usually the result of a process of adapting to cultural patterns, and only the more sophisticated moderns, aided by social science, have learned to be aware of themselves in connection with this cultural process. Generally people don't see culture, they see by means of it, and their perceptions and values are largely the results of enculturation that has taken place so continuously and so covertly that, as Margaret Mead has said, they are like a fish in water who sees through water but is unlikely to discover the water itself.

When a nation commits itself, as the United States has, to a yearly budget of 70 billion dollars or more to support a huge military establishment, with interconnected industries and universities working on military contracts, and with more than two-thirds [14] of its technical and scientific talent working on military projects, that nation is likely to be highly involved in the military outlook. The involvement tends to bring into being the kind of world which is forecast. Saul Friedman found that the RAND Corporation, the civilian research organization of the Air Force, "has done little positive research toward ending nuclear confrontation because of the belief of RAND's leading thinkers that the theory of 'mutual invulnerability' is a positive way to peace." [15] One could hardly expect the hired brains of the Air Force to challenge the assumptions on which the future of the Air Force depends, yet Friedman shows how RAND's prophecies helped *create* policy and actually escalate the arms race.

"In 1957, when the Russians launched the first Sputnik, RAND predicted the Soviet Union would embark on a crash ICBM program which would leave the United States on the short end of an intercontinental missile gap by 1961. As a result the United States began a crash ICBM program. As it developed, the Russians did not increase production of their ICBM until 1961, *when it became evident to them that the United States had an overwhelming superiority. The RAND prediction, wrong, as it turned out, precipitated another round of the arms race."* [italics mine.]

The fall-out shelter program of the early '60's held the same danger. It failed to take into account that American policy is one cause of the cold war. If Americans had embarked on a massive civil defense program they might have deceived themselves into feeling secure, therefore they might have become even more convinced that there is no need to work toward the changes necessary to bring about the international control of nuclear weapons and an end to the source of the danger. Civil defense could easily have become a reinforcing factor in creating the conditions which would precipitate thermonuclear war. To rely on a nuclear deterrent and yet also to rely on survival by crawling into holes in the ground is to behave in a way which would increase the likelihood that the shelters would in fact need to be used.

The strong and narrowly successful drive in 1969 by the Nixon administration for an Anti-Ballistic Missile revealed the persisting locked-in commitment to nuclear threat systems and the entire military metaphysic. In spite of the fact that the proposed ABMs had very low levels of effectiveness, and in spite of the theoretical contradictions — that if deterrence systems would effectively deter there wouldn't be any need to have a system to shoot down incoming missiles — the President and his administration proposed and won a new level of economic and technical commitment to the arms race.

C. Wright Mills seems to have been right when he said that "the immediate cause of World War III is the preparation of it." [16] Though there may have been instances when preparation for war has led to temporary peace, in the main, the historical evidence is that preparation for war is usually the path to war. [17] Preparation for war carries with it an outlook which involves attitudes and actions built around a perception of other nations as military threats. Other nations may indeed be military threats, but the long-run procedure for avoiding atmoic war is to build up cooperative structures, such as a strong United Nations with an international police force. When a nation bases its future on a military deterrence theory, it easily becomes obsessed with the strategies, materials, and techniques of war. Short-run military defense takes priority over long-run peace goals and long-run goals are perpetually deferred. A cycle of fear produces more militarization, which leads to new heights of fear and new levels of militarization. In the post-atomic world this produces a nation much too similar to lemmings scurrying ever more rapidly after their leader, consoled by the collective comfort of mass conformity, and heading blindly to the cliffs overlooking the sea and to impending disaster.

C. VIOLENCE IN THE AMERICAN WAY OF LIFE

Most habits can probably be changed, but some are more persistent than others, especially when they are part of a long established pattern. In the American way of life there is considerable distance between the creed and the deed. Americans typically defend the idea of peace, but the 1960's were characteristic of this gulf between ideals and performance. Editors, politicians, union leaders, businessmen, and many others were talking about peace and yet accepting or advocating repeated cycles of war escalation in Vietnam. This behavior was more interwoven with a cultural predilection for violence than most Americans would like to believe. It was not only such predictable groups as the Daughters of the American Revolution who cried for increased bombing, but sample polls, prior to 1969, consistently revealed that most Americans wanted to intensify the violence.

Violence has by no means been an exclusive prerogative of military establishments; it has permeated the civilian culture from the earliest period of American history. Early Americans burned women at the stake as witches. For years the American Indian was subjected to merciless slaughter and repeated violation of governmental promises. One of our founding fathers, Lord Jeffry Amherst, favored genocide for the "savages" and suggested that the final solution was to send the Indians blankets infected with smallpox. [18] Much of our land was literally stolen from the Indians. The perceptive Frenchman DeTocqueville wrote that Americans had many unusual virtues but that "one encounters a complete insensitivity, a sort of cold and implacable egotism when it's a question of the American Indigenes (Indians) . . . It's the same pitiless instinct which animates the European here as everywhere else." [19] This same insensibility may have assisted American support of the B-52 bombings of rural Vietnam villages in order to kill "suspected" communists. As an American Air Force pilot said on a television interview in 1965, the people they killed in Vietnam were "like vermin, like animals. You don't worry about it. They aren't really human — you just shoot them down."

American ethnocentrism places the White Anglo-Saxon Protestant at the cultural center, for an accident of American history brought WASP immigration first. The further the cultural distance from the early American in-group, the easier it has been to give people semi-human or even non-human status.[20] Africans were bought like chattel and chained in the holds of ships to die enroute to the land of liberty or to arrive as slaves.

We were often devious when it fitted our interests. Though it is commonplace for Americans to claim that they have never committed an act of aggression, it requires gross ignorance of the past to be serious about such an assertion. We invaded Canada in 1775 and in 1847 and made, as Arnold Toynbee says, "sweeping annexations of territory at Mexico's expense."[21] We took over Hawaii by force, with the use of Marines,[22] promoted the Spanish-American war in Cuba, annexed the Philippines and other former Spanish colonies, and obtained rights to the Panama Canal by nefarious means.[23] This was presumably sanctioned by "westward expansion" or "manifest destiny," but if other nations had done it we would call it imperialism. Commager says we believed in "New World innocence and Old World corruption . . . and our irresponsibility was really a form of [belief in our own] moral superiority." Contemporary foreign policy includes this same "double standard of morality . . . we justly condemn Nazi destruction of Rotterdam and Warsaw, cities that were not military objectives, but we conveniently forget that we were chiefly responsible for the senseless destruction of Dresden — not a military target — within a few weeks of the end of the war, with a loss of 135,000 lives."[24] And we decided that the Nuremburg Tribunal should apply the "principle" of war crimes only to the vanquished, not to the victors.

We also atom-bombed Japanese cities, with a high loss of lives, not for military but for political reasons, and two other Japanese cities were scheduled for similar incineration. Since then we have kept our Central Intelligence Agency busy trying to subvert governments and revolutions on a global scale, even those in the "free world."[25] The CIA planned the Cuban invasion, and its power was not reduced as a result of this military-political disaster. We flew U-2 spy planes over Russia, China, and Cuba, but we would have made a self-righteous and bellicose protest if these countries had done the same to us. The U-2 flights were terminated, not because of respect for international law, but because they were replaced by the superior technology of spy-satellites.

A serious recent event in our history of self-righteousness has been the violation of the Geneva Accords and the United Nations Charter through our intervention in Vietnam to support a South Vietnamese military government which was largely created by American power as an instrument of our own foreign policy. Aggression has not been a continuous American policy, but it has occurred often enough to make pronouncements of innocence tantamount to admissions of ignorance.

By exaggerating the aggressiveness of nations which are not pro-American and by exaggerating the peacefulness of our own behavior, we reveal our hypocrisy to people not conditioned to accept American nationalism. Felix Greene quotes a Chinese historian who recently said, "It is ironic, isn't it, that it is the United States, of all countries, that is saying we are aggressive and expansive? China doesn't have a single soldier outside of China — not one. And how many does America have — a million and a half."[26]

Fortunately there is the brighter side of American history. We finally eliminated the sordid institution of slavery, although we failed during Reconstruction to guarantee Negroes entrance to the system. We accepted many of the destitute from Europe and some from Asia, but even this benevolence was morally tarnished by the industrial need for cheap labor. After undermining our own conception of a League of Nations, we helped create one of the most hopeful instruments of peace — the United Nations, about which we have, nevertheless, remained ambivalent. We reduced its strength through support of the veto power and the Connally Amendment in which the United States rejected the jurisdiction of the World Court to decide whether a dispute was a national problem. The amendment violated international law and weakened the United Nations.[27] We were not ready to yield national sovereignty to an international agency even on questions of international conflict. We called on the United Nations only after our unilateral excursion into Vietnam was not proceeding satisfactorily. Nevertheless, when the negotiation conditions suggested by U Thant were not to our liking, they were ignored.

The Marshall Plan and the policies of the Japanese occupation have probably been high points of postwar policy, but even the Marshall Plan involved fear of a postwar economic decline in the United States and included some of our perennial anti-communist obsessions. Yet it did indicate our capacity to engage in constructive activity, whatever the motive. For many years after the creation of the American republic we inspired people throughout the world as a symbol of self-determination and democracy, but our contradictory and often violent behavior is rapidly dimming international faith in the American creed. Our deeds have too often been unrelated. Howard Beale, an historian specializing in the history of American freedom, pointed out that "the tendency to coerce conformity and to resort to mob violence against the dissenter from popular opinion has been much greater in American history than men have realized or like to admit."[28]

Do the central activities of a nation reveal its values? Assuming that they do, Norman Cousins asks the question: "What is it that man makes or grows or processes more of than anything else in the world?" The answer turns out to be, "Explosive, obliterative forces . . . It takes the form of fission and fusion bombs of varying sizes and potencies. They have been accumulating in man's storehouse and are primed for instant use. These explosives represent the destructive equivalent of 100,000,000,000,000 pounds of TNT. This comes to 28,000 pounds of explosive force for every human being now alive. All the foods and medicines and books and clothes in the world do not amount to 28,000 pounds per person, nor even a substantial fraction of it." [29] And what country leads the world in the production of explosives? The United States. Russia is second, and other nations are rapidly joining the "nuclear club." However, the United States seems determined to retain its "leadership".

American television, the vast wasteland nominee, offers the programs it claims Americans want. These consist largely of harmless trivia, occasional information programs often placed at unprofitable hours, and seemingly endless hours of violence, with intermittent commercials. Compared with the British Broadcasting Corporation, American television is much more restrained where controversial treatment of sex or religion is concerned. But with violence, Americans clearly have the lead. One British broadcasting executive stated: "Our viewers just don't go for extreme violence." The British code, in fact outlaws "violence for its own sake." [30] American television "entertains" with programs involving perpetual conflict between people which is resolved through shooting and killing. The six-shooter justice of the frontiersman is perennial TV material. But increasingly electronically embellished programs intensified the free world-communist world stereotype by teaching the viewer that "our" more clever use of violence always produces victory.

Violence is not limited to entertainment in the United States, for we have achieved in real life one of the highest, if not the highest, homicide rates in any of the "civilized" countries. The frontier folkways of television are still practiced in sections of the United States where guns are used to compensate for the lack of civilization.

American police have often been free-wheeling in their use of guns. The British "Bobbies" are not even armed. The police rioted and clubbed (but did not kill) demonstrators and non-demonstrators during the 1968 Chicago Democratic National Convention. They carried on a murderous conspiracy against the Black Panther Party in 1969. For years the police have been a major cause of civil liberties violation by their unlawful enforcement of the law. They have often served as armed representatives of the middle class illegally applying repressive violence to lower class minorities.

Yet Americans have no basis for claiming an exclusive achievement in their obsession with violence. German behavior in World War II, particularly with respect to the Jews, set an all-time high for barbarism and violence. The Japanese, at least in their Samurai traditions, have carried on the history of brutality. The Japanese initiated the war with the United States, but did so by bombing *military* installations. The Americans terminated the war by mass incineration of *civilian* populations, even though our officials knew such action was not necessary to end the war.[31] According to Tristam Coffin ''there is no evidence that we are peace-loving or ever have been. We have taken whatever we wanted by force if need be . . . we have maintained a righteous air, contending that we have committed mayhem and felony with the purest motives. This is a result of our Puritan inheritance, which requires proof that God is on our side in every expedition and sanguinary action.''[32]

Though comparative national propensities for violence are difficult to measure, American traditions and the current outlook would seem to give the United States a leading position. For most countries this would not be a matter of grave concern, but when the willingness to use violence is combined with self-righteousness and backed by massive technology, it is a formula for making the future dangerous and uncertain.

The most hopeful indication that the American way might change is that by the latter 1960's more attempts at honest understanding were occuring. From such unlikely sources as a government sponsored commission (The Eisenhower Commission) came the following statements:

Engrained in American life is the tradition, even the love of violence . . . Americans have always been given to a kind of historical amnesia that masks much of the turbulent past. Probably all nations share this tendency to sweeten memories of their past through collective repression, but Americans have probably magnified this process of recollection, owing to our historical vision of ourselves as a latter-day chosen people, a New Jerusalem.[33]

From this same study of The History of Violence in America the following explanation was offered:

The operational philosophy that the end justified the means became the keynote of Revolutionary violence. Thus given sanctification by the Revolution, Americans have never been loathe to employ the most unremitting violence in the interest of a cause deemed to be a good one.[34]

People can change if they look at themselves in the mirror and decide that they don't like what they see. To do this requires both a mirror and an honest willingness to face up to what it reveals.

D. Toys of Terror

In each society the fantasies and games of its children are connected with the traditions of the society, for the games serve as part of the process of enculturation. They provide continuity with the past and preparation for the future. Eskimo children play snow games and Polynesian children play

65

water games. American children play many kinds of games, but in recent years nothing has exceeded the popularity of war games.

War games have not always been popular in American society. The games reflect the historical period, but they not only reflect, they also enculture the children to the values of that period. They intensify the norms that prevail.

Before the mid-nineteenth century, geographical games and card games and children's magazines were commonplace. By mid-century, factory toys became common. Most of them were exercise and educational toys such as blocks, rocking horses, and other symbols of a peaceful world. But toy guns increased after the Civil War, and increasingly the more technically fascinating weapons were modeled into toys for American children. Other events than war were reflected in the toys, and a toy pistol was called the "Chinese Must Go" model, reflecting the then current agitation for exclusion of Chinese laborers.

The early twentieth century became even more of a military age, and war toys became more popular and more imaginative, and during the Spanish-American war, such toys greatly increased. By the time World War I was over, war toy manufacturing was a flourishing industry. Mc-Clintock's history of war games refers to Milton Bradley's "At the Front," a game which contained "soldiers which are to be taken out and fired at . . . Each soldier stands until he is shot and then he falls like a man." [35]

Later during the more peaceful 1920's, thousands of children were questioned in a study designed to reveal their favorite play activity. Playing soldier was low on the list. Such games as tag, horse, hide and seek, marbles, and skipping had gained more popularity. [36]

But during and since World War II there has been a resurgence in war games, and they are now a common experience in the lives of American children. Children's war games are big business, and manufacturers display American ingenuity in providing ever more realistic and intriguing toys. Sears Roebuck, and Company is typical of the mass merchandisers who sell such toys. Sears' products may not always reflect dominant American values, but their selections probably provide a rough index of typical American interests. Each winter Sears publishes a special Christmas catalogue, and a sizeable section is devoted to children's toys. The selections provide an indication of the modern American conception of a Merry Christmas.

The new games, in a changing world with changing values, are given the spotlight. During the ascendency of the Vietnam war, the lead game in the 1964 catalogue was *RISK*. It is described with the statement: "Build up armies in strategic spots to invade continent after continent in a bold plan to conquer the world." To the American youth who wishes more detail, the game is said to be "based on Napoleon's 'balance of power' concept during the 1800's. Players place armies on all 42 territories. Then a roll of one or more dice pits army against army. Attack neighboring territories with each turn . . . control entire continents to gain more armies. Win by occupying every territory on the board.''

WAR GAME-CONFLICT is also offered to provide an equally worthy use of leisure time. It is described as ''all-out war as you move ships, planes, guns, over land and water areas. Roll back enemy forces, capture his home circle.'' And since there are competing companies in the American toy market, there are competing games. *COMBAT* offers the relatively unexciting prospect to ''free your men, occupy enemy headquarters to capture his six soldiers. Meet face to face in combat . . . spin to see who is captured or escapes.''

War not only can be fun, it can be played in so many different ways. The game *STRATEGIC COMMAND* adds new interest with magnetism. ''Move ships, planes, tanks on 192 grids . . . magnetically repel opponent',s forces behind 19 inch panel. Use strategy to capture headquarters.'' Another game, *STRATEGO,* invites the player to ''Pull your rank' and you challenge enemy's pawns and try to capture flag . . . It takes smart tactics and cool nerves to win. Guess how the opponent's men and bombs are placed as you advance across the field. Each pawn's rank is hidden. When challenged, one with lesser rank drops out.''

A young player more interested in history than current affairs is offered two games titled ''American Heritage.'' One is called *BATTLE CRY.* It is a Civil War game described as ''Command Union or Confederate armies. Force enemy into pocket or capture troops to win.'' A World War I game called *DOGFIGHT* says ''Be an Air Ace of World War I. Put plane on patrol, shoot down enemy planes.'' All of the games suggest minimum ages for embarking on this war fun. A few suggest age seven, but since some games are appropriate only for the more mature, they go as high as age 10 for the appropriate minimum age.

A good game not only can develop a child's mind but also his perception. One game called the *SPY DETECTOR* says ''test your skill in deduction . . . get 'Hot Top' clues, track down foreign agents — then question them . . . An enemy agent has stolen our secret Rocket Fuel formula. Round up 24 witness suspects. Examine their testimony to see if answers are true or false. Analyze the guilty one and you're promoted. Become Top Secret Agent and win'. A different suspect is guilty each time.''

Sears did not restrict American youth to somebody else's rules for war. There were 33 other pages in this catalogue which include military uniforms, models, and mock equipment so that creative, active American youths who want maximum identification with war can come as close to reality as possible.

Americans need not fear that they will lose their international lead in manufacturing children's games based on the most up-to-date forms of violence. Other countries are way behind. A leading German toymaker offers children models of ancient Roman soldiers, and Mignon, the French toy manufacturer, does not offer anything "more contemporary than a seventeenth century musketeer."[37] By comparison, good old American know-how has developed a game sold by the Nuclear War Game Company of Downey, California, in which players "attempt to gain world domination" with cards representing hydrogen bombs of various megatons. Other cards represent delivery vehicles such as the B-70 bomber and the various types of missiles. Victims of an attack attempt to defend themselves with anti-missile cards. The spinner offers such directions as "lethal doses of radioactive gamma rays kill another 10 million" and players are told "If the 100-megaton bomb explodes a nuclear stockpile, a super chain reaction starts which destroys all countries, the earth itself and the entire solar system . . . everybody lost." This game is, of course, a logical culmination of the technical progress of the last few years. At least it speaks of a reality that most people avoid. The tragedy is that it is designed not for governments seeking peace but for children seeking thrills.

There is no certainty that children who play the war games of today will be aggressive war-oriented adults of tomorrow. But there is enough evidence to justify serious concern. The effects of the experience of violence raise the probability of subsequent aggressive acts.[38] A clinical professor of psychiatry has stated that war toys are dangerous and that "it is imperative for man, if he is to survive, to psychologically alter the outmoded value systems which serve to make war psychologically palatable and to replace them with others which have greater adaptive value."[39] And Benjamin Spock has stated "It is not that pistol play and television violence will lead to war or that the absence of these will prevent war. It is attitudes that are crucial. When we let people grow up feeling that cruelty is all right provided they know it is make believe . . . We make it easier for them to go berserk when the provocation comes."[40]

Most toy manufacturers, their eye on their profits, disregard the educational consequences of war toys and claim that war games are merely the result of the adult world of violence and are irrelevant as a cause. The Mattel Company, Louis Marx and Company, and Hassenfeld Brothers and their "GI Joe" have helped civilian neighborhoods become realistic battlegrounds for American children, and if there is any remorse it isn't evident in their profit and loss statements.

Many Americans have grown up with war play, dividing themselves into Americans versus the enemy, and practicing the deadly arts of war with the encouragement of American industry. War games have been part of the education of young America. Such education has not been merely realistic adjustment to future roles, it has been a way of helping create the realities of tomorrow out of the fantasies of today.

Yet the seemingly total emersion in war has produced its own reaction, and the peace movement has included organized effort to stop the trend in war toys. The Lionel Toy Company and a few others have dissociated themselves from war play. Lionel's advertising in 1965 was based on the theme "Sane Toys for Healthy Children." Creative Playthings, a manufacturer in Princeton, New Jersey, sells no military toys. Quite the contrary, this manufacturer has selected a variety of toys designed to provide physical and intellectual growth without encouraging children to become warriors and to have contempt or insensitivity for human life. Their catalogue says, "Toy materials are used by children to play-act roles in the larger society — the family, the community, the country, the world. The adventurer, pioneer, and explorer roles that relate to building a better society, whether at home, in the jungle, in the depths of the ocean or in outer space, can replace the unimaginative exact replicas of military equipment."

The decline in the popularity of the Vietnam war has brought increasingly effective public pressure against children's war games. Judged by the 1969 Sear's Toy Catalogue, the pressures have finally become effective. Whereas war was the overwhelming theme in the 1964 catalogue, the 1969 catalogue devotes no more than two percent of its items to war toys. Clearly this reflects one of the few hopeful trends that have arisen from rising national indignation. It suggests, however, that it is possible for an awakened society to finally extricate itself from the culture of war.

E. MILITARY CONSCRIPTION: FORCED TO KILL

American youth continue to be forced to serve in the Armed Forces for a period of two years. Though the conscientious objector classification has been slightly liberalized, draft-age youth can be and are being sent to countries such as Vietnam to kill whomever the President designates as an "enemy." Often the American draftees are wounded, crippled, or returned in coffins.

It is claimed that the draft is necessary for American national defense, therefore individual freedoms must be forfeited to meet the emergency. The same practices and the same arguments are used by totalitarian governments to justify using the absolute power of the state. In a totalitarian society it would be expected that policies would be based on the principle that the end justifies the means. In a society ostensibly dedicated to democratic principles, the destruction of individual freedoms becomes justified only when the society is actually in such peril that survival must be given priority over democratic values. Has American survival actually required the draft, or have American freedoms eroded until the draft has become part of a semi-totalitarian American way of life?

General military conscription was adopted in World War I, terminating with the end of the war. It first appeared during peacetime in 1940 as a preparatory measure, soon to be used to fulfill the manpower requirements of World War II, which for Americans began with the bombing of Pearl Harbor in 1941. The 1940 act expired in 1947, after the end of World War II. It was renewed one year later with a 21-month draft requirement, but lack of manpower needs permitted draftees to be released by the end of 1949. The 1948 act was to expire in 1950, but with the invasion of South Korea, Congress extended it to 1951. Then a new conception of the draft was introduced. Labeled *The Universal Military Training and Service Act,* it was passed in 1951, and it authorized peacetime conscription as national policy. Its "universal" aspects were a misnomer, but it placed a claim for a period of *eight* years on the lives of young men between the ages of 18 and 26, involving two years of active duty with the remainder of the time in a reserve subject to recall in case of emergency. [41] This was an attempt to institutionalize the idea of a "military obligation." It was apparently successful, for it became commonplace for people to say that young men are "obligated" to serve in the military. Until the Vietnam protests there was little sign of organized revolt by American youth. Unaccustomed to anything except a cold war outlook, young Americans of the post-World War II era accepted the draft with stoic resignation (until the mid 1960's). Prior to the Vietnam War it was as heretical to speak against the draft as it had been heretical to speak for it prior to World War II.

So-called "universal" training, ostensibly to serve national defense, was extended and modified slightly in 1955. Congress extended the draft in 1967 during the Vietnam war and showed little sign of considering conscription obsolete or immoral. Though the draft is labeled "universal" it provided exemption to a scientific-technological elite — those who held jobs essential to the military-industrial complex. [42] College students were exempted from the draft prior to the 1969 lottery, with future hopes for exemption based on their preparing for the "right" jobs. National examinations were given to college students for draft exemption to channel the selection of the scientific-industrial elite, by using the examination to favor students competent in math, science, and engineering. It is clear that the new privileged class has consisted of those who have had the privilege of not being drafted to "serve" their country.

Of the total draft age youth, not more than half of those eligible were taken, but in May, 1966, Senator Russell, Chairman of the Senate Armed Forces Committee, said he would try to get every young American to have at least six months of military training (presumably, women were to be exempt). Political pressures have been developing against the injustices of an ostensible "universal" military training law which in fact takes a higher percentage of lower class youth than middle or upper class, because exemptions discriminate against the lower class. The main quick road to exemption for all classes has been marriage and fatherhood. It may never be known how many children have been conceived or how many marriages have been created to aid a young man to avoid the draft. In a period of American history when divorce rates are high and when planned parenthood is needed, the draft has given a grim meaning to "planning."

Policies which encourage the creation of human life to escape military servitude are one of the many grotesque by-products of conscription.

In response to the flagrant discrimination in conscription laws and draft board practices, a lottery procedure was developed in 1969 in which the fate of youth was more equitably established by the roll of government dice. (Birthdates actually.) A more equitable procedure is being used to implement an immoral law.

The causes of our conscription policy are complex. Some motivations are based on fear of future wars, some on the desire to back political alliance with a show of force. Underlying these external concerns is the belief in threat systems and a pervasive, often paranoid anti-communism. There are the economic concerns interwoven into our military-industrial complex. Taking men off the labor market aids unions by reducing the supply of labor. It also takes pressure off the government to keep unemployment rates low, for the draft syphons off manpower, particularly through a draft that has been rigged to draw heavily on the lower classes.

The American economic system has never been prosperous and stable for a sustained period of time on a non-wartime basis. World War II "solved" the great depression, and the United States has used military pump-priming ever since.[43] The draft with attendant military spending provides contracts and profits for business and helps to keep the stock market high. Also, the military system itself provides so many jobs and positions of power that millions of Americans have a vested interest in a large permanent military establishment, and they possess ample ability and purpose to contrive justifications for the continuation of the establishment. Many have become so much a part of the military value system that they can argue with conviction for a continuing, even a burgeoning military. Our own civilian President Truman was so enamoured of military values that after World War II he had favored a peacetime draft as an instrument for *educating* the civilian population. He advocated universal military training, giving the following reasons in his *Memoirs*.

"This was not a military training program in the conventional sense. The military phase was incidental to what I had in mind. While the training was to offer every qualified young man a chance to perfect himself . . . in some military capacity, I envisioned (sic) a program that would at the same time provide ample opportunity for self-improvement. Part of the training was calculated to develop skill that could be used in civilian life, to raise the physical standard of the nation's manpower, to lower the illiteracy rate, to develop *citizenship responsibilities* and to foster the *moral* and *spiritual* welfare of our young people." (italics mine.)[44]

President Truman was not a voice in the wilderness. He was in the mainstream of a developing trend to which he gave impetus. The escalation of military values has continued, and many civilians have come to think of the military establishment as not merely an instrument of defense but a guiding light for transforming civilian America.

Other reasons for advocating a draft are more subtle and indirect. It is probably insignificant that those who have the power to determine draft laws are themselves ordinarily exempt from the draft. The old decide whether the young should be sent to the battlefield. This is an ancient system whereby some of the youth are sacrificed to honor the chief and to bring glory to the tribe. Those who parade the glorious shrines of our dead soldiers are typically those who are the most aggressive and chauvinistic and ready to urge policies which create more shrines.

The elders who force the young into a military system sometimes treat the process as a type of puberty rite, opening the portals to "manhood." A similar phenomenon is seen in secret clubs and fraternities. Those who have been inducted, hazed, and even brutalized and have tolerated the system and become part of it can retaliate for their own suffering by perpetuating the sadistic cycle and remain exempt from the consequences of their actions. Immorality is increased by systems that separate people from the consequences of their actions and make irresponsibility easy. Power hierarchies and the remoteness of consequences (as the release of bombs by a B-52 bombardier) increase the barbarism of modern life. How different it would be if those who declared war would also be expected to fight it, particularly in direct confrontation with the enemy, using only bayonets. The platitudes uttered by modern politicians would suddenly be converted into the awful reality of what they had foisted upon themselves. How morally simple it is by comparison to send out battle orders from Washington or to press a button sending an ICBM, never having to witness nor to accept the responsibility for the consequences of such an obscene act.

Those who possess what Bertrand Russell calls "statistical imagination" can translate the vast numbers of people killed by modern weapons into human terms. These are the citizens who are least adapted to the role of an impersonal technician of death and destruction. Those who protest against conscription because of their understanding of the effect on human life are among the most valuable members of a society. Many show more courage through their protests than they would by submitting to the draft. The protester in American society risks physical violence and therefore displays physical courage. So may a soldier in combat. In every war, including Vietnam, the instances of physical courage become legion. But moral courage is possibly a higher type of courage, and it is apparent that many who are protesting against conscription are among those most devoted to democratic freedom and to a belief in the worth and dignity of the individual, American or non-American. The central moral commitments of a democratic philosophy are often abandoned by those who have accepted nationalism and an in-group, out-group psychology.

Protesters against military conscription have been accused of hypocrisy by men like Marine Corps Commandant Wallace M. Greene, Jr., who think young men should serve their country in some type of service role. The Commandant does not seem to be aware that many young men do not object to all *public* service but to *military* service. It is the nature of the military demand which is rejected. Paul Booth, former secretary of the Students for a Democratic Society, has said, ''We are fully prepared to volunteer for service to our country and to democracy. Let us see what happens if service to democracy is made grounds for exemption from military service. I predict that almost every member of my generation would choose to build, not to burn; to teach, not to torture; to help, not to kill.''[45] The idealism of the many young people who have volunteered to work in the civil rights movement and the Peace Corps attests to Mr. Booth's statement. Yale psychologist, Kenneth Keniston, after an in depth study of anti-military and anti-war youth, indicated that *moral* concern lay at the heart of their protests.[46]

It is hardly to be lamented that the new generation has become critical of an ethnocentric morality common to the old generation, whose members often seem to make geography the basic criterion of morality. If a young man kills overseas he becomes a ''patriot,'' but if he kills within his own country he is a ''murderer.'' The new American heresy is the belief that there is something wrong with killing.

The draft, like other by-products of militarism, is dangerously erosive of democratic values. Young people have been uncertain whether their use of civil liberties will cause their draft board to punish them by early conscription. (In Jan. 1970 the Supreme Court stopped this practice.) American youth must carry draft cards at all times like criminals or citizens of a totalitarian society. When it was revealed that Negroes in South Africa must carry identification cards subject to continuous police check, it was obvious that the demands were part of the totalitarianism of the South African government. Yet young American men are being put in a similar role as creatures of the state, subject to continued police scrutiny. A driver's license to identify demonstrated competence to perform a privileged activity is defensible in a democratic society. But a draft card which says ''the law requires you to have this card in your possession at all times'' is like a civilian ''dog tag'' designed to keep the adult male population under surveillance until age 44, long after they are even draftable. The card is one more encroachment by the state on what used to be called democratic freedoms. It is part of the new militarized America and also part of the accoutrements of a police state. The entire draft is probably unconstitutional, violating the thirteenth amendment prohibiting involuntary servitude, but as yet the Supreme Court has not tested the draft laws.

Is there *any* justification for the American draft? It is often stated that it is required to serve *manpower* needs. This is becoming remarkably commonplace language, yet it is dangerously close to the logic of totalitarian ideology. First, it assumes that an elite has determined for the rest of us what our needs are, therefore what our manpower needs are. Secondly, it justifies the potential use of police coercion for the solution to any manpower shortage. What if the principle is extended to include "manpower needs" in other sectors of society? What of shortages of doctors, teachers, or construction workers of a highly hazardous nature? Why not draft people to be doctors, teachers, and to construct dangerous buildings? Obviously this becomes clearly an instance of totalitarian state power over individual choice. It is said that a military draft is needed because the job is dangerous, but there are jobs where the danger is greater than in the military and yet people are attracted by compensatory salaries and other prestige factors, not by conscription. And in time of a thermonuclear war a civilian resident of Los Angeles or New York City may be in as much or more danger than a soldier.

It is sometimes claimed that the military is inevitably so odious that it is not possible to attract men on a voluntary basis. Yet no systematic attempt has been made to find out. There are many ways of making military life less repulsive, and the salary that is normally offered for inducement, which is comparable to migrant farm wages, would pre-determine a manpower shortage in any other American vocation.

Ralph J. Cordiner, president of General Electric, headed a committee of the Defense Department on military pay and proposed changes which he insists would make it possible to reduce active forces by 10 percent and also abolish the draft. The Gates Commission also provided a plan to eliminate conscription. There are professional soldiers who concur and who dislike coercing men into the military, not only for the demoralizing results, but because so few conscriptees stay in the Armed Forces. If the world's richest nation prefers to coerce rather than accept public responsibility for paying what is necessary to attract men into the military on a voluntary basis, it has embraced a remarkably indecent public policy. The draft of 1940 was undertaken at a time when the American economy might not have been able to afford payment necessary to induce sufficient numbers of men voluntarily. This is no longer the case, and it may even be true that a voluntary military would cost less than one based on coercion, because the turnover rate would probably be markedly reduced.

If the draft is not the only way to acquire manpower, can we justify it because conditions are so critical that we have to choose *between* our freedoms and our survival? This may have characterized conditions in World War II, but the United States Commander-in-Chief has not suggested that the Dominican Republic was ready to take over Florida or that the Vietnamese constituted a serious threat to the state of Hawaii. We did not enter Vietnam for national defense but rather for national "interests" as defined by a power elite.

One neglected reason for eliminating the draft in a democracy is that public support of foreign policy can more easily be validated. The numbers of men willing to fight in the Armed Forces would be expected to be high if people are convinced that the cause is important and the policy is right. Even though a draft was instituted in World War II, men were generally willing to fight against the brutality and inhumanity of fascist Germany. The cause was supported and the policy was supported, but how convinced were Americans that they needed to invade the Dominican Republic, and how convinced were they that we should fight a war in Vietnam? What constitutes a good foreign policy in a democracy? Must it not be policy that is worthy of uncoerced public support? Would American foreign policy be strengthened or weakened if it were made to stand the test of explanation, justification, and the support of citizens willing to back it up by direct action? A draft can produce the appearance of support for what is in fact poor policy. Why did Americans so willingly support American policy in World War II, and why have they been so much less willing to support American policy in Vietnam? Would Americans need to be drafted if invasion was imminent and national defense was really necessary?

If Americans have come to believe that whatever an American president decrees must be right, they have acquired the attitude of a totalitarian citizenry. For a president to *be right* as often as possible, he must have the benefit of the processes by which policy can be validated. It seems significant that the more that Americans have come to understand American policy and its consequences in Vietnam, the more disenchanted they have become. This disenchantment would have had more impact on foreign policy if it had produced diminishing military manpower.

There is one basic moral question connected with the draft which is not subject to pragmatic analysis. Does a government have the *right* to force a citizen to kill? If one man kills another for anything except self-defense it is considered a despicable crime and labeled murder within national laws. But if a citizen of one country kills a citizen of another country, is the act any less a *moral* violation? Does national law supersede all moral consideration? In a totalitarian system national decrees are supposed to supersede all other moral and ethical considerations. Yet the Biblical mandate against killing was intended to supersede political decree.

Humanists such as Mulford Sibley hold an ethical commitment which puts priority on mankind. Sibley says, ''I must regard myself first as a human being and only secondarily as a national. I must, on occasion, be unpatriotic — in the professional's terms — if I would be ethically responsible.''[47] To the religious man as to the humanist there is a limit to what the state has a right to ask of him. Asking a man to kill, even more, forcing him to do so is to prevent individuals from being responsible for the most serious act a man can commit. The undermining of human responsibility undermines a democratic system. Americans recognized this after World War II and applied the principle to the Nuremberg trials. Have we now decided that it is only Germans and defeated nations who can commit ''crimes against humanity''? We expected Germans to show individual responsibility against inhumane orders. Yet when Americans are drafted and forced to drop bombs on Vietnamese villagers, do the Nuremberg principles not apply to us?[48]

By 1970 the resistance to the draft had become widespread. Draft card burning, conscientious objectors, and jail sentences in lieu of conscription were rapidly on the increase. Young men were increasingly going to Canada and Sweden, some to transfer their citizenship rather than submit to the draft. Like many of their forebears from Europe, they were refugees from a militaristic homeland.

The first hopeful change in national administration outlook came from President Nixon who advocated during his 1968 campaign and even after he was elected that he would try to terminate the draft when the Vietnam war was concluded. A few congressmen concurred, but by 1972, the president and the congressmen showed more interest in developing an equitable draft than in abolishing it.

Critics of a volunteer army often say that they most fear a totally professional army. There are many cases in the history of other countries where professional armies have taken power away from civilian governments. But this concern overlooks the fact that elimination of the draft would have no real affect on the power structure of the American military system, since it is currently a professional army in the officer ranks. Draftees almost always are assigned as enlisted men, and it is only the officers, especially the Pentagon brass who have sufficient control over the military system to produce a political coup. The Pentagon power structure is not weakened by having a draft; it only provides an abundance of cheap labor (slave labor) to be ordered by those who have the power.

The draft has had one positive value—it has helped politicize American youth. Their opposition to the draft is one of the elements in the current generation gap. The draft is a political target for youth on both the political left and on the right; it provides some cohesion between disparate political factions. It is not likely that the draft will continue to be as invulnerable to change as it has been in the last two decades, for it will be a major target for change among the youth it has helped politicize.

F. THE AMERICAN CONTRIBUTION TO THE COLD WAR

The popular version of the cold war is that Russia was aggressive and expansionistic after World War II and that communism, under the control of the Kremlin, was bent on subversion and international conquest. The western democracies, of which the United States is leader, have tried to strengthen the ''free'' world and to encircle and contain first Russia and now China with our military might. With two allegedly opposed ideologies (American-freedom vs. Russian-totalitarianism), the atomic bomb, the hydrogen bomb, and the expanding delivery systems of the United States have been used to keep a knife poised over Russia if she should be overly aggressive. Each side is seen to take a tough line toward the other and to live under continual tension, conflict, and suspicion. It is a form of war, but it is not overt hot war. It is considered the best we can hope for until the *Russians* cease to be aggressive. It is believed that it is the Russians who are really to blame for the cold war. American policy, according to this formulation, is designed only for the avoidance of war and unnecessary killing.

It is comforting to any nation to believe that the fault lies merely with the other side. It has helped Americans continue the arms race with the self-righteous belief that they were not responsible for aggression or for the cold war. But as more of the record is being made clear it is becoming increasingly difficult for informed Americans to have a basis for such innocent self-righteousness. The "cause" of something as complex as the cold war may be difficult to identify. Americans have difficulty understanding why the Soviets should be suspicious of them, but they forget their own invasion of Russia and Siberia during the Russian Revolution.[49] They use Lenin's warlike utterances to convince themselves of Russian military aggressiveness, failing to understand the differences between ideological aggressiveness and military aggressiveness. As Fred Neal points out, "Nowhere in the whole body of Soviet Marxist theory is there the implication that the Soviet Union, for ideological or any other reasons, should itself initiate a war."[50] The Marxist idea of "world domination" is a political prophesy based on a historical theory, not a plan of world military conquest. Americans have had difficulty separating communist ideology from fascist ideology, for the latter did include plans for aggressive military expansion, especially under Hitler and Tojo.

One can be sure from the outset that there have been *many* causes for the cold war. Russia is very much a part of the international process and shares responsibility, particularly during Stalin's rule. But Americans share more of the blame than the popular version of the cold war suggests.

Plans for the cold war were taking shape even before World War II ended. A carefully documented study of American policy during 1945 by Gar Alperovitz, titled *Atomic Diplomacy: Hiroshima and Potsdam,* has shown how the United States under President Truman dropped the atom bomb on Hiroshima and Nagasaki in order to enforce American *political* demands on the Russians. The crucial point is that two cities of human beings were incinerated, (and two more were scheduled) not to stop the war and to save American lives, according to popular belief, but rather to demonstrate American might to the Russians in the belief that the Russians could be forced to accept American policies.

Alperovitz has pieced the events together with careful documentation, so that the evidence comes as close to being irrefutable as can be expected of a study of this type. The burden of proof is now very much on those who would claim that the atom bombing of Japan was *militarily* necessary. His study shows that the Russians (even under Stalin) were trying to live up to the Yalta agreements, formulated while Roosevelt was alive, but that Truman, as president after Roosevelt's death, wanted to reinterpret the Yalta agreements to "shift to a tough policy aimed at forcing Soviet acquiescence to American plans for Eastern and Central Europe."[51]

Virtually no one in a position of authority thought there would be need for a land invasion of Japan with possible loss of many thousands of American lives; however, this was the popular belief created by President Truman and offered by the press. Even if Truman had wanted to hold a military club over the Russians, there was no need to demonstrate the terrible power of an atom bomb, a spectacle of callous horror which was reminiscent of the Nazi barbarism that was even then being revealed to a shocked world. Dr. James Franck, a member of the panel of nuclear scientists working on the atomic project, presented a report in June (the bomb was dropped in August) "suggesting a technical demonstration of the bombs." It strongly recommended against a surprise attack upon Japan. The report said, "Russia and even allied countries which bear mistrust of our ways and intentions . . . may be deeply shocked by this step."[52]

Alperovitz shows that Truman unquestionably knew that the atomic bomb was *not* needed to end the war in Japan. B-29 raids had inflicted mortal damage to Japan, a March 10 raid on Tokyo resulted in 124,000 casualties. The bulk of the Japanese fleet had been sunk and the Japanese Air Force was almost impotent by early in the summer of 1945. The Japanese knew that defeat was inevitable and they were actively trying to negoitate a surrender, hoping to retain a few minor concessions. *The American Joint Chiefs of Staff informed the president that the war with Japan was virtually over and that atom bombs were not needed to terminate it.* General Eisenhower had told the American Secretary of War, Henry Stimson, that he had

> grave misgivings first on the basis of my belief that Japan was already defeated and that dropping the bomb was completely unnecessary, and secondly because I thought that our country should avoid shocking world opinion by the use of a weapon whose employment was, I thought, no longer mandatory as a measure to save American lives. It was my belief that Japan was, at that very moment, seeking some way to surrender with a minimum loss of "face" . . . . It wasn't necessary to hit them with that awful thing.[53]

The President and his *civilian* political advisors, says Alperovitz, did not seem to have Eisenhower's "grave misgivings." They had political objectives in mind and were willing to use an atomic bomb on a civil population to strengthen their hand in negotiation with the *Russians*. This may well be the most cynical and barbaric act in the history of American politics. The civilian heads of government, not the military, were anxious to use the most devastating instrument of war ever developed, not for national defense, but for political leverage. The grim episode is punctuated by the fact that this cynical strategy did not work. Some concessions were made at first by the Soviets, but Truman took a demanding, unnegotiable position when it was confirmed that the atom bomb was operative; it "gave him an entirely new feeling of confidence."[54] James Byrnes,

Truman's Secretary of State, was as anxious as Truman to change the cooperative relationship Roosevelt had with the Soviets, and when the atom bomb was a reality he prepared to meet with the Soviets with a new confidence. He wrote that it was "in a very real sense, a test of strength." At the London Conference Byrnes pressed demands to revise the power relationships in Bulgaria and Rumania, and Molotov refused. The meeting broke down, and even Byrnes later wrote that "our attitude was a shock to them."[55] Alperovitz says, that "postwar Soviet-American tension must be dated from the London Conference."[56] Even Secretary of War Stimson later admitted that he was wrong in "the attempt to use the bomb to gain diplomatic objectives."[57] Instead of the atom bomb policy being an instrument of American-dictated peace, as Truman had expected, it instituted a military foreign policy based on the threat of atomic annihilation. Stimson later admitted that it was "by far the more dangerous course."[58]

Though Alperovitz's careful and detailed documentation should be read to get an accurate sense of the continuity of the events, it is surely clear that Truman, Byrnes, and Stimson were amply aware that it was *not* necessary to bomb Hiroshima and Nagasaki to end the war in Japan. The Chiefs of Staff had told them, and they did not disagree. But from the inception of the atomic bomb project they had *assumed* that the atom bomb would be used on Japan and they did not question the policy. General Arnold was instructed by the Joint Chiefs to "reserve four cities for attack by the atomic bomb."[59] The decision to use a devastating military weapon as a club in international politics embarked the U. S. on a course from which it has never extricated itself. This was Truman's "tough-minded" approach, his conception of how to prevent World War III. It led rather to the arms race, which more reflective men foresaw, and to an *increasingly precarious* "balance of terror" that has characterized subsequent Russian-American relations. Truman was skeptical of international systems of armament control, and his own Acting Secretary Joseph Grew believed that "a future war with Soviet Russia is as certain as anything in this world can be certain."[60] At the same time Walter Lippmann was taking a very different view, stating "that the best that was possible was an accommodation, a *modus vivendi,* a working arrangement, some simple form of cooperation, and that in demanding more than that we have been getting less than that."[61]

Stimson, more than Truman or Byrnes, showed realistic awareness of the consequences of a military-based foreign policy. He "did not believe the new power could be used to force the Russians to accept American terms on diplomatic issues. He thought such a course would inevitably lead to an arms race."[62] He believed that "some form of international control of the new development was absolutely essential. If control were not achieved, the results could be disastrous. 'In other words,' he told Truman, 'modern civilization might be completely destroyed.'"[63] A scientific panel, which included Robert Oppenheimer, pointed out after the atom bomb was dropped that even more powerful thermo-nuclear bombs instead of fission bombs could be produced, and the panel's "unanimous and urgent recommendation" was that these developments be under international control.[64] Byrnes, however, responded to Oppenheimer that the "proposal about international agreement was not practical and that he and the rest of the gang should pursue their work (on the hydrogen weapon) full force."[65] American policy became committed to a position it has been tied to ever since. "Peace" became a function of the American capacity to annihilate with atomic weapons, and it soon turned into a mutual capacity to annihilate as Russia developed nuclear weapons. It turned into a multiple capacity as other nations developed thermonuclear bombs and missile systems, and we increasingly live in a "community of fear" as Harrison Brown calls it. If the Americans had concentrated on building cooperative and even international systems of armament control in 1945 instead of taking the self-appointed role of judge, jury, and policeman for what has increasingly become the entire world, we might now live in a world built on an entirely different basis. Instead we have had continuous arms escalation and a cold war with Russia, and we must bear much of the responsibility for both.

It is a serious mistake to assume that it has been only the professional soldier who has been committed to a reliance on military power. Militarism has been a central committment of civilian heads of government since World War II. Unlike our civilian heads of government, the reaction of *some* of the heads of the military, such as General Eisenhower, Admiral Leahy, and General Curtis Lemay, to the plan for needlessly atom-bombing the Japanese was a feeling of "revulsion."[66] Lemay's jingoistic views on Vietnam hardly put him in the class of reluctant bombers. His opposition to using the A-bomb on Japan is, therefore, all the more striking.

The cold war and the atomic-based foreign policy continues. John Foster Dulles, Secretary of State under Eisenhower, developed the political strategy of nuclear "brinkmanship" which put the U S. in a position similar to American boys who play "chicken" by driving cars toward each other in a head-on collision, the winner being the one who jumps off last, moments prior to collision and death.

During the Eisenhower era, Walter Millis pointed out:

> "Khrushchev has not in fact threatened us with intercontinental missile war. Rather he has utilized Russia's scientific and technical triumph to appropriate the American policy, announced by John Foster Dulles in 1954, of maintaining 'a capacity for massive retaliation at times and places of our own choosing.' . . . Our diplomacy, while always clothed in the moralistic phrase, has been basically military in character — filled with 'offensives,' 'psychological warfare,' 'positions of strength,' 'flank attacks,' the 'deployment' of our economic power, and so on."[67].

David Horowitz has completed the picture of American cold war involvement from 1945-1965. Horowitz destroys the myth that the U.S.S.R. did not demobilize while the U. S. did and also the myth that Russia was a likely military threat to the U.S. following World War II. His thesis is that American politics has been mainly responsible for the cold war and for the nuclear arms race, and he supports his thesis with persuasive documentation.[68]

Though the American government is still committed to ''containment'' policies and a belief in peace through ''deterrence,'' some of those who were early champions of a military based foreign policy are now convinced that the policy is a mistake. George Kennan, who helped formulate the containment policy after World War II, delivered lectures over the BBC during the spring of 1958 which were strongly critical of the assumptions underlying American policy. One of America's leading authorities on the Soviet Union, he stated that ''until we stop pushing the Kremlin against a closed door, we shall never learn whether it would be prepared to go through an open door.''[69]

There was uneasiness among the more perceptive congressmen, and in 1958 the Senate Foreign Relations Committee probed American policy to help develop necessary change. James Warburg, a writer on foreign affairs highly esteemed by Adlai Stevenson, stated before the committee:

> ''I have no doubt that (Secretary Dulles) will say once more as he has frequently said in the past, that he sees no reason to reconsider any of his basic premises and policies. If so, he will in truth outdo the Roman Emperor Nero, who is said to have fiddled while Rome burned but who, so far as I know, never appeared before the Roman Senate to deny that the city was on fire . . . The blunt truth is . . . that if the West does not quickly put its own house in order, it will be too late . . . to negotiate.''[70]

The Republicans and the Democrats often disagree on domestic issues, but an ironic aspect of American politics is that there has been substantial agreement on basic foreign policy throughout the cold war. In this one area of agreement we might have been much better off if there had been more disagreement, but a common outlook based on suspicion and the threat of military power has provided the main area of political agreement. There have been minor anti-cold war achievements such as the agreement with Russia on the cessation of nuclear testing. The irony is that Eisenhower dismissed the idea of a test ban as absurd when it was proposed by Adlai Stevenson during his presidential campaign against Eisenhower. Groups such as SANE had pressed for a test ban and the public was beginning to get information on the danger of fallout. Finally even Eisenhower conceded to the need, and a test ban treaty was negotiated.

President Kennedy appeared to be aware of the need for stopping the cold war and agreed with Khrushchev on the need to work for general and complete disarmament. But it is one thing to make a verbal claim for peace and quite another to back it by deeds. Harold Taylor, a member of the Peace Research Institute, has questioned the credibility even of Kennedy's professions of peace by pointing out that the Kennedy budget requests to Congress ''reflect a continuing reliance on military deterrence as national policy, with an *increase* in military appropriation and a pittance for arms control and disarmament.''[71] Taylor points out that the Swedish delegation to a seventeen-Nation Disarmament Conference in Geneva proposed in 1962 a plan to draw up a test-ban treaty which was flippantly dismissed by the head of the American delegation, even though it was a carefully-worked-out proposal by intelligent scholar-diplomats. Kennedy also authorized the Cuban invasion, helping to undermine the United Nations and international law, and he continued Eisenhower's support of American involvement in Vietnam. Even so he showed more restraint than President Johnson, who moved foreign policy to the political right, [72] even though the American public had opposed *Goldwater's* belligerent Vietnam proposals and had provided him with a resounding defeat in favor of Johnson in the 1964 election. To the surprise of many of his electors, Johnson took over the Goldwater position on Vietnam and rapidly escalated and expanded the war in Vietnam, and then invaded the Dominican Republic to support a right-wing military government. Under the Johnson administration, the world became more divided, for the detente between Russia and the United States which gained headway under Kennedy was threatened by American involvement in Vietnam. The Nixon administration reduced ground forces in Vietnam but increased the air war, and by 1972 had managed to invade Cambodia and Laos and to drop more bombs on Indochina than the total dropped during World War II and the Korean War. American policy continued to be a major factor in making the world more dangerous. In the name of national defense we have stockpiled hydrogen bombs and other armament, virtually predetermining that the Russians and the Chinese must do the same thing. We have turned priorities upside down, relying on military solutions to political problems instead of finding political solutions to military problems.

G. THE POVERTY OF A MILITARY BASED AFFLUENCE

Norman Cousins has described a discussion with a businessman who feared that a war with Communist China would ''crack the market.'' He felt differently about the war in Vietnam. It was ''just right — not steep enough to risk nuclear war but deep enough to maintain the present level of government defense spending and feed the present industrial boom.'' A few days after the conversation Norman Cousins read about peace feelers from North Vietnam. The final editions of papers that day ''carried related stories that stock prices at first tumbled in response to the peace scare but then rallied near the closing as later news disclosed that the 'feelers' were not of recent date and had already been discounted. Thus reassured, investors returned to the buying side.''[73]

As uncomfortable as it is to admit that the Marxist prophecy about the profitability of war in a capitalist society has been a very real part of contemporary American society, it is undeniable that during and since World War II, the great American prosperity has been primed by huge military spending. And pride in a low unemployment level during the Johnson administration coincided with escalation of the war in Vietnam and increased draft levels. American Presidents proudly report, in the yearly State of the Union report, that the gross national product has risen. But it leaves one to ask not only what the difference would be if peace broke out but also what *kind* of gross national product have we? With the contracts for ICBMs and napalm, it is in a truly grim sense a ''gross'' product.

One particularly interesting study has raised serious questions about even the economic consequences of a war-based economy. In *Our Depleted Society,* Seymour Melman strongly suggests that a war-based economy produces not only moral decay but even economic decay. Described as ''an economic audit of the price that America has paid for twenty years of cold war,''[74] his study raises serious questions about the *quality* of recent American economic growth. For instance, where is American technical talent channeled? Can we really call it prosperity if a substantial percentage of Americans build instruments of human destruction? Melman points out, with extensive documentation, that ''while United States research programs for civilian purposes are grossly understaffed, and many industries do virtually no research at all, more than two-thirds of America's technical researchers now work for the military.''[75] The Department of Defense employs directly nearly four million people and has total property exceeding $171 billion. Much of the effort is to ''increase'' *overkill* capacity, a goal which itself places no little strain on human sanity.

Because of the failure to replace plant and capital to better serve civilian domestic and international markets, American industries are declining in their realative *rate* of productivity, compared with most other industrial nations. They are also becoming less and less capable of competing on international markets. Americans are increasingly finding themselves dependent on foreign business ''know-how,'' so that a more appropriate revision of the claim of American business leadership might be ''good old American knew-how.'' The Italians are having to help Americans learn how to make typewriters, and many American companies are having to lean on foreign manufacturers to continue. Sewing machines, railways, ships, and electronics are among the examples cited of increasingly non-competitive industries. By 1963, ''the United States had reached the position of operating the oldest stock of metal-working machinery of any industrial country in the world.'' American industries are so largely dependent on military contracts that they have not been disciplined by the more exacting demands of an international market. Even domestic markets are increasingly lost to foreign manufacturers. Since military production has priority, the anomaly of huge statistical increases in gross national product goes side by side with the continuation of over a fifth of the American population living in poverty. When the Vietnam war is over, American poverty can be expected to continue if a costly military system is retained.

The first priority economic objectives of a massive military machine has sidetracked other objectives into second, third, and even no-priority positions. While war production increased from 1950 to 1963, physicians in practice in the United States dropped from 109 doctors per 100,000 population to 97 per 100,000. More is spent on the military than is spent for education. While natural resources are poured into military production, we are depleting economic resources and natural beauty that are scarce, even irreplaceable. The domestic residue of war production often consists of little more than increased air pollution and more contaminated water supplies. This was happening under the euphemistic labels of both Republican and Democratic administrators, including President Johnson's "Great Society." Harold Lasswell more accurately called it the "Garrison State."[76]

Melman points out how Americans have exported this policy of decay by selling surplus military production to other countries and particularly by exporting military aid to underdeveloped countries. These programs have often diverted badly needed civilian technical manpower in those countries in military technical roles, undermining economic development. When the United States closed down some military installations in Turkey in 1963, it released 2000 badly needed Turkish technicians into the civilian economy.[77] Much of what we call foreign aid is really military aid, which helps keep the underdeveloped countries undeveloped.

While American energy and resources are diverted into the channels of war production, the inevitable arms race produces increased national insecurity instead of security, and many domestic needs fall into neglect even though the economy continues to expand. Melman has called attention, with supporting facts, to the mythology of a military-based prosperity. It is well known that war psychology produces moral decay, only recently has there been more awareness, aided by Melman's studies, that war production produces economic decay.

During the later 1960's, as the Vietnam war dragged on, the *peace* news increasingly produced a rise rather than a drop in the stock market. The resistance to the military-industrial juggernaut may increase as people become more aware that the war is an economic burden to most people and that only a small group profits by war. This is especially likely to be understood as the domestic neglect in social and environmental conditions requires the kind of enormous expenditure that has been reserved for the military for the last quarter of a century.

H. HAVE WE A SUICIDAL CULTURE?

Senator Fulbright tried in 1964 to shock the nation, or at least national leadership, into sanity by pointing out that "when we refuse to believe some things because it displeases us or frightens us . . . the gap between fact and perception becomes a chasm . . . . The divergence has in certain respects been growing . . . . Our policies are based at least partly on cherished myths."[78]

The national behavior that makes sense in one historical period may not make sense in another. In the many foreign wars Americans have fought they have been able to feel "successful" primarily because they were able to win. But success through winning by military means only encourages reliance on future military solutions. It encourages separation of means from ends rather than concentrating on the processes by which any meaningful success can be developed in the post-atomic age. Pre-atomic unilateral military solutions have been increasingly rather than decreasingly used by the United States, even though the United States helped form the United Nations twenty years ago to provide a system of multilateral mediation. Within a three year period the American government engineered a military invasion of Cuba, invaded the Dominican Republic, and became extensively involved in Vietnam. Some years preceding we encircled Russia and China with air bases and missile sites under a unilateral "containment policy," thereby commiting ourselves to the role of global sheriff with over 3,000 military installations around the world.[79] Yet when the Russians tried to establish missile sites next to us in Cuba, an act comparable to our own, we thought it necessary to risk nuclear brinkmanship to force a showdown withdrawal. What if the Russians had followed the same policy with respect to American missiles in Turkey?

Fred Neal questions what he calls the "American psychology of non-acceptance" by pointing out that "only a psychological situation in which we did not really accept the reality of the U.S.S.R. can explain our inability to realize that we cannot undertake or threaten action Moscow considers provocative without there being a Soviet reaction." When Khruschev warned that countries establishing American rocket sites or permitting U-2 flight bases were participating in provocative action, the U. S. State Department listed these statements under the title of "Soviet Threats of Destruction Against the Free World."[80] We carried the attitude of non-acceptance to Communist China with U-2 provocations and Vietnam border skirmishes. China may not prove to be as tolerant of us as the Russians have been, when she possesses nuclear retaliatory power.

Instead of developing an increasingly stronger system of international law and an international system of conflict management, we have apparently never overcome the rugged individualism of our frontier experience where men often made their own law and were skeptical of cooperative systems. We seem also to have carried our nineteenth century social Darwinism into the 20th century world scene, building morality around the power either to win or be a paternalistic rich uncle, precluding communication as equals. We are one of the most self-righteous nations in the world, and though we pride ourselves for our practicality, we are in a basic sense profoundly absolutistic and anti-practical. We ordinarily adhere in national economic policy to doctrinaire theory, and in international foreign policy we often stand for meanings of freedom and human rights which ignore the culture and the history of other people. Our ideological narrow-mindedness has equaled or surpassed that of many communist nations, and has encouraged us to try to reorder the world in our own image. Our unilateral invasions have weakened the United Nations and have helped undermine international law.[81] We piously pronounce our belief in world peace, but have we become so reliant on pre-atomic modes of behavior that the requirements for peace in the post-atomic world elude us? If so, we have many of the characteristics of a suicidal culture.

Our very economic success may be our own undoing. While our technology has won wars and made us enormously wealthy, it has also made us smug and conservative and reliant on the cultural orientation of the past. We continue to amass thermonuclear power and build delivery systems even though we have long passed the point of overkill. We responded to each military and political defeat in Vietnam by expanding the war, and by extending the war close to the border of China, we have dangerously toyed with the possibility of war with China, stimulating the militarization of the Chinese. It was as though the lesson of Korea had been so soon forgotten.[82] While lemmings are driven to their destruction by seemingly uncontrollable instincts; Americans seem to be victims of their own culture, blissfully enjoying the fruits of their technology while using it in a manner which often appears as compulsively suicidal as the instinctual lemming.

Is American culture rooted in a common human nature which predetermines warlike behavior? This was a common view difficult to refute prior to the development of the behavioral sciences.[83] Now we know there is no *genetic* basis for war, for people have developed cultures which are peaceful and non-aggressive.[84] However, there are *cultural* reasons for being aggressive. Yet culture can be changed, though it is ordinarily resistant to change. People usually continue their habits persistently until they are certain they will no longer work; fundamental change usually comes from a reaction to a crisis situation. The great depression altered American political-economic policy. Similarly, we could expect World War III to alter American foreign policy.

But can American foreign policy be altered substantially before World War III, while the human race is still intact? American behavior in Vietnam offers little basis for an affirmative answer. There has been the same fanatical anti-communism, the same reliance on military power, and the same belief in American superiority and invincibility which has characterized the American outlook for years. Erich Fromm says there are many elements of pathology in American political thought.[85, 86] One is *paraonoid delusion,* which involves the belief that something is after us. The condition is pathological in that objective conditions are not weighed

86

to identify realistic probabilities. A possibility is converted into an obsessive certainty. The ideological challenge of communism is converted into an obsessive belief that military world domination is the aim of all communists.

The second pathological mechanism Fromm lists is *projection.* This involves the transference of what is actually one's own problem. "The enemy appears as the embodiment of all evil because all evil I feel in myself is projected into him. Logically, after this has happened, I consider myself as the embodiment of all good since the evil has been transferred to the other side. The result is indignation and hatred against the enemy and uncritical, narcissistic self-glorification."

The third common form of American pathology is *fanaticism,* a quality revealed by a "passion which has no warmth." The fanatic "does not really feel anything since authentic feeling is always the result of the interrelation between oneself *and* the world . . . he has the illusion of 'feeling' of inner excitement, while he has no *authentic* feeling . . . he has built for himself an idol, an absolute, to which he surrenders completely." Keeping in mind these pathology classifications, it is interesting to contrast people at the center of the American establishment with those who never quite made the grade. Our leaders have been Harry Truman rather than Norman Thomas; John Foster Dulles rather than George Kennan; Dwight Eisenhower rather than Adlai Stevenson; Lyndon Johnson rather than J. William Fulbright. And how should Dean Rusk, Secretary Laird and Richard Nixon be classified? Surely there are more responsible men available to control immense power.

Americans have shown a failure to recognize leadership appropriate to the atomic age, but "the times, they are changing." The rumblings of protest have become louder and more effective. At first they were barely audible — a few asking for a "sane nuclear policy", though virtually no mass media then admitted the possibility that the defense policy of the establishment might not be sane. Then came the tragic barbarism of the Vietnam war — the napalm, the defoliation, the massacres, and the dumping of 3 times as many bombs as was dropped in World Warld War II — to support a corrupt military government that lacked the support of the people. Increasingly even the mass media could no longer support the war. The Vietnam Moratorium march on Washington late in 1969 became the largest gathering of American dissenters in history.

Increasingly the road to sanity has become a viable option. The courageous dissenters have often been those very types of Americans whom earlier congressional committees labeled as un-American. Sometimes they have been at the fringe of political power, willing to become the heretics of the establishment rather than the loyalists. Fulbright, Morse, McGovern, Gruening, and Nelson were among the early senatorial leaders of this dissent. By 1969 many others were admitting the error of Vietnam, and the pervasive militarism of American society was beginning to be questioned both in Congress and in the mass media. Even a retired Marine Corps General, David M. Shoup, decried the frightening rise of American militarism, [87] and by mid-1969, more congressmen and other members of the establishment were beginning to say what had already been said for years by the anti-war protestors.

If the dissent continues — and the flagrant political, military, and moral absurdity of the war in Vietnam has fanned the flames of discontent — a new America may be created, possibly able to develop a humane and responsible policy suitable to the atomic age. This is probably the period of greatest crisis in American history, and the outcome is by no means clear. A new leadership may emerge, more concerned with human life than with military-based policies. Or the old leadership may continue, using the outmoded values of another era, heading the human race toward disaster.

CHAPTER V

TEACHING MILITARY VALUES
THROUGH AMERICAN SCHOOLS

Though American educational institutions are complex, they are part of a larger society which has changed more by drift and accommodation than by conscious design.[1] The schools, equally, have been plagued by vagueness and uncertainty. In a changing world a rigid commitment to a single purpose would make no sense, but schools typically have difficulty even making sense of what they are currently doing. Plans for the future are usually highly tenuous or non-existent. Even the authority roles are so unsettled that responsibilities are seldom defined with sufficient clarity to permit one to establish accountability. In such an environment it is not strange to find that schools become a sort of supermarket for special interest groups where every and any conceivable demand, from creative art to throwing hand grenades, may be made on students in the name of education.

American schools, particularly below the college level, have generally yielded to dominant pressures, reinforcing the status quo and insuring a continuation of their power.[2] Without a clear philosophy of education or a rationale of objectives, this kind of homeostatic politics has been understandable. But it means that bureaucratic politics instead of responsible foresight tends to guide American education. And so when the first Russian Sputnik flew over and our military superiority was thought to be challenged, the schools soon became instruments of the military-industrial complex by having national crash programs in math and science. Some states passed legislation to get the schools to propagandize anti-communism, otherwise the near-dormant social studies remained dormant.[3]

PRE-MILITARY EDUCATION

Bertrand Russell has said that American schools tend to drive the tack where the carpet was last year. Much that is now taught may have had some relevance to the nineteenth and early twentieth centuries, but in a world where World War III is an ever-present possibility, many schools are not only anachronistic but dangerous. They confuse distinctions between democracy and nationalism. They try to get students to accept a concept of citizenship more appropriate to a totalitarian society. And they generally ignore critical inquiry into the great issues of our day. Thus they contribute to World War III.

The political and economic influences of any warfare state tend to transform institutional education at all levels, but a war-oriented education is not always the result of outside pressures. Many American educators favor military values, though they may classify them under a different label. When schools include ROTC programs, they directly and overtly advance militarism; however, they may advance militarism just as effectively by teaching aspects of a military outlook indirectly and covertly. A military outlook, with its special beliefs about authority, loyalty, citizenship, identity, and human nature, insinuates itself into much that is transmitted through American schools.

A child's first encounter with militarism in school may be with his Junior Police officer peers. The external form of military order is often stressed in Junior Police Organizations, which use students in both elementary schools and high schools to police traffic for other students attending school. Students participate on a voluntary basis and work with the police force to control crosswalk traffic. The goals are commendable, but programs often emphasize military procedures such as close-order drill and become similar to the ROTC in their use of authoritarian regimentation.

A child may next be influenced by the Scouts.[4] Though the Scouts are organized outside the public schools, they are often idealized in the schools as model citizens. They often serve in the Junior Police corps, and they often lead flag salutes in PTA meetings and school assemblies. Not only are the Scout organizations semi-military in their use of uniforms and drill, but they also indoctrinate a narrow ideological conservatism similar to Armed Forces ideology.[5] Though they are somewhat more internationally oriented than in past years, they are still a politically conservative, semi-military special interest group. They have every right to existence in a democratic society, but the value systems of such special interest groups should not be uncritically accepted as educational models for public schools.

Few schools are guided by any carefully examined educational theory. Most of them operate on the widely held belief that schools should transmit the culture and adjust students to conventional values of the society. Rather than being "life-adjustment" education as this orientation is sometimes called, it could now more accurately be labeled "death-adjustment" education, since it results in transmitting a pre-atomic education in a post-atomic world.

Examples of such education are commonplace. In 1967, teachers in Montana offered examples of their "citizenship" education through their state journal.[6] Citizenship was characterized by such activities as children wearing badges stating, "I'm proud to be an American." Boy Scouts presented the flag and joined the Girl Scouts in reciting their oath of duty to God and country. Children sang patriotic songs and received an explanation of the historic background of the American flag. Students sent letters to their congressmen telling them "why we should be proud to be Americans." Programs of nationalistic songs were presented which received approval from the local American Legion. Nationalistic poems were written, and the credo of the Freedom Foundations was used as the standard of citizenship for some of the schools.

The dominant theme was nationalism. An absolutist, conservative ideology was indoctrinated as a unanimously accepted fact rather than as a belief held by a segment of American society. The Montana Education Association proudly published reports of these educational achievements, and Montana is quite representative in its educational outlook. In the modern world, such quaint simplistic political faith lays the background for later cynicism, now widespread among America's young adults, for it ignores actual problems and offers no way of coping with complex modern reality.

Failure to distinguish between different meanings of patriotism and citizenship is part of the problem. A totalitarian value system demands that people define themselves by uncritically accepting an imposed pattern of behavior and belief, while a democratic system aids people in defining themselves through critical participation. When a totalitarian value system, as characterized by military institutions, is taught in American schools, the justifying logic would have to be: "America is a democracy, therefore whatever Americans do is democratic."

In the name of democracy students are often encouraged to be ethnocentric, unquestioning, and dutiful toward constituted authority. Whether the authority is democratically constituted and whether it makes sense is often disregarded. In the name of democracy children parade the symbols of national superiority. Our schools, especially at the elementary level, make a fetish of the flag salute, as though it had some relationship to citizenship in a democracy. Required salutes are actually compulsory loyalty oaths which attempt to substitute uniformity of belief for the voluntary choice that underlies democratic patriotism.

In the early development of nations, nationalism can be an expansive, integrating force which carries people beyond tribalism and localism by broadening their basis for identification.[7] At the turn of the century, when immigrants came to the United States from a variety of countries, American nationalism had a unifying influence, as is the case now with many newly developing countries. But for developed nations like the United States, internationalism and supranationalism are the integrating forces. Not only does it offer expanded experience and a broader conception of life, but it has become a prerequisite to survival in an age when weapons must be internationally controlled if nations and the people in them are to continue their existence.

In a rapidly changing world a narrow prescriptive education smothers the very creative abilities which are vitally needed to solve the critical problems of a nuclear age. Much of American education is merely culturally irrelevant, but some is mis-education, which actually handicaps children's ability to participate intelligently in the modern world.

JUNIOR ROTC

The National Defense Act of 1916 not only expanded the regular

ROTC but also created a program of military training for *high school students,* called Junior ROTC. The first programs were initiated in 1919-1920, during the fervor of nationalism and militarism accompanying World War I. By 1925 there were about 42,000 high school students in the programs. School districts made individual requests if they wished to be included in the program. The Army supplied equipment, materials, uniforms, and instructors. Another program, called the National Defense Cadet Corps Program, was instituted at the same time. Schools were required to finance this program except for textbooks, training equipment, and surplus rifles, which were supplied by the Army. Schools have never shown much interest in Cadet Programs, though they have made more requests for Junior ROTC, with its free instructors, than available funds would allow. Ever since its creation in 1916 critics have challenged the supporters. Nationalism continued to be so strong after World War I that the militarists had minimum opposition, but later in the 1920's and particularly during the 1930's, anti-militarists became more vocal and in some cases moderately effective.

In the 1930's the private Committee on Militarism in Education and its chairman, Professor George A. Coe, working with Edwin Johnson as secretary, provided organized opposition to rising militarism. *Harper's Magazine* pointed out in May 1933 that these ''two young men in a dilapidated back room furnished with chairs that must be sat on carefully lest they fall apart'' were able to hold back some of the pressure to militarize. ''All over the country the military propagandists are constantly harassed by this Committee and unquestionably would like to put a bounty on the heads of the two young men.'' Writing in many periodicals, including leading education journals, and working in opposition to specific programs of ROTC expansion, the Committee provided a valuable service in informing people of issues they might have otherwise overlooked. They first concentrated on the most brutal aspects of militarism, and they were able to get changes in military manuals and to stop bayonet practice in ROTC. In 1935 Edwin Johnson wrote that the ROTC programs were antithetical to the ideals of a democratic society and promoted instead ''compulsion, (and) tribal dogmas believed with an intensity which saves them both from the exactitude of scientific scrutiny and the tentativity and skepticism which mark the scientific temper.''[8] In 1939 he raised the increasingly relevant question of whether militarism is a ''a cause of war in the sense that it contributes to the cultivation of that outlook of mind which is essential to the perpetuation of the war customs among and between nations.''[9]

The educators, with their characteristic caution, tended to avoid the value issues and stayed within the safer area of ''research.'' Studies were conducted to determine the consequences of military training. In 1929 William G. Carr, later executive secretary of the NEA, made ''A Plea for Research into Our Military Training.''[10] Some apparently heard the plea, and a few studies were made. One in 1935 indicated that college ROTC students showed more "obedience to an unthinking kind of patriotism,"[11] but it was not clear whether the courses caused this or whether "ROTC selects and holds men already having this idea of patriotism."

However, one study of students at a private military academy indicated that the academy had not made the students more "eager for war or for a chance to use their military knowledge."[12] And in a Junior ROTC program in a "southern" high school, where there is a tradition of reverence for the military, the hardly remarkable discovery was made that "military training attracted a superior group of boys." The investigators also concluded that there was "no evidence . . . That military training will make boys more militaristic in attitude or interest."[13] They failed to add that the instruction must therefore be ineffective, for it failed to achieve even what it set out to achieve. At the present time, the limited research available suggests that there often is no measurable change in students who take ROTC, and it is common to find so-called "educators" who support ROTC because they claim "it doesn't hurt anyone."

But some studies have measured what might be considered negative effects. Gaylord Nelson, now U.S. Senator from Wisconsin, made a study to "discover how high school boys electing ROTC in preference to physical education (a common option) might differ from the majority who accept the normal physical education program." He found that the ROTC students were more socially withdrawn, more shy, stronger in their belief that obedience and respect for authority are the most important virtues, more often lacking in individuality, less competitive, and more in need to hide behind the strength of the group.[14] It appears that voluntary ROTC attracts such students and perpetuates these characteristics rather than produces them.

Junior ROTC and Cadet programs have been permitted to expand gradually until there were about 72,000 male high school students continuously enrolled in them by World War II, and by 1960-1961 there were about 60,000 in Junior ROTC and 20,000 in the Cadet Corps program.[15]

High schools have had a choice of whether to make these programs required or elective. By 1964 there were 254 high schools, public and private, with Junior ROTC programs.

Junior ROTC Programs in 1964[16]

	Public H.S.	Private H.S.	Total
Required	46	9	55
Elective	198 (2 in Canal Zone)	1	199
	244	10	254

Junior ROTC programs had been frozen at this level since 1947, but in a remarkable performance, all this was changed by the 88th Congress in the fall of 1964. In spite of the fact that it was authoritatively stated by the Defense Department that "there is no direct military requirement for this type of program,"[17] Congress passed H.R. 9124, which provided funds for making the program *nearly five times as large.* Congress also knew that Junior ROTC "does not produce officers." In fact the Department of Defense even pointed out that the program is a *hindrance* to current national defense because it "requires the services of some 700 active-duty military personnel. Expansion of this program to a level of 1200 schools would require the services of 3,300 active-duty military personnel as instructors, and an additional 200 as supervisors. We do not believe that this constitutes a wise use of military resources, considering the enormous demands of our defense, and the related priorities that must be placed on funds and personnel."[18]

Yet in spite of the program not being in any sense vital to national defense, in fact a hindrance by keeping instructors unavailable for normal use, Congress passed the bill by a high majority. It had been promoted by Senator Russell, Chairman of the Senate Armed Forces Committee. Though he was not connected with the Health, Welfare and Education Committee, he argued for the bill for *educational* reasons, saying:

"I confess that there is no immediate and direct military need for this training. But it does teach some semblance of discipline . . . It does provide some basic training . . . It does assist in maintaining the health of the young men. It does enable us to get the young men out and drill them. If we need anything in this country today, we need something that would instill some semblance of discipline, some respect for order, and some respect for authority in the young manhood of America. I can conceive of no more beneficial piece of legislation than this."[19]

Senator Gaylord Nelson from Wisconsin led the opposition, saying:

"Why in heaven's name should we require the Departments of the Army, and the Departments of the Navy and the Air Force — which do not now have such programs — to accept up to 1,200 schools when the Department has said that the program is of no value? . . . To argue that the purpose of the program is to instill patriotism, discipline, and improved health is one kind of an agrument. If that objective is so important, let us introduce a bill which would achieve that result."[20]

Apparently the majority of American Congressmen were not really so interested in that result as they were in the expansion of military influence in the schools. It is difficult to identify human motivation, but it may be relevant that Senator Russell's state of Georgia had seven elective Junior ROTC programs and *23 required* programs. In 1964 this was nearly half the total number of required programs in the *entire* United States. In addition the state of Georgia, with the help of their Senator, has been "crammed with nineteen military installations — so many that an indiscreet general is said once to have remarked, 'One more base would sink the state.' "[21]

According to democratic theory, our civilian government is supposed to use the military but to keep it under control. One would assume, therefore, that members of the Armed Forces Committee would be something other than militarists in civilian clothing. Yet it would be hard to imagine a more useful Senator for serving the *military* than Richard Russell. He and the Congressmen who supported him helped extend the "military-industrial complex," which President Eisenhower had already warned about, with the addition of a military-*educational* complex. Senator Russell, the people who elected him (many of whom have taken compulsory ROTC), the Democratic Party that placed him on the Armed Forces Committee, and the Congressmen who supported H. R. 9124 must take a considerable share of the responsibility for this major step in expanding the area of military influence into public education and thereby into the America of tomorrow.

The Senate Hearings on H.R. 9124 were revealing of the groups that had a special interest in expanding military influence in American high schools.[22] A group of military officers representing the National Association of National Defense Cadet Corps Schools were anxious to get more federal support for private high schools which are classed as Military Institutes, and so they supported the legislation. Then a representative of the American Legion strongly supported the bill saying that these military programs in the high schools are of the "utmost importance to the future of this Nation."[23] The American Legion had recently passed a resolution backing the legislation, and their spokesman at the hearings said:

"In addition to its military value, ROTC training is of inestimable value in teaching leadership, confidence, citizenship, and patriotism. This instruction is simply not available in any other academic department."[24]

Next the representative of the Reserve Officers Association (accompanied by the Director of Air Force Affairs and the Director of Army Affairs) argued in favor of Junior ROTC. Then a statement by Congressman Kastenmeier of Wisconsin was inserted in the records. This was the only vigorous statement of opposition to Junior ROTC offered in the hearings. The Congressman pointed out that Junior ROTC

"Would actually reduce combat effectiveness of the Armed Forces by draining manpower away from more essential functions. (He added that) The principle sponsor of this legislation in the House indicated on the floor that the expanded junior ROTC program was conceived as a way to achieve in America what Hitler and Castro have achieved in the mass molding of German and Cuban youths . . . If I understand this prescription correctly, it means that the lesson to learn from Hitler and Castro is that they are more to be emulated than despised."[25]

He added that the ROTC programs made demands on already over-crowded space and pressures to study legitimate subjects, and added that Junior ROTC is "in many ways incompatible with the goals of a growing and open society."

However, Senator Inouye of Hawaii, who labels himself a liberal, was strongly supportive of the program.[26] He has been one of the many American legislators who are members of the Armed Forces Reserve. While supporting military projects (as a civilian member of the Senate Armed Forces Committee) and military budgets he has been involved with other Congressmen in a conflict of interest as real as a member of Congress who hold substantial stock in a company and makes political decisions favoring war contracts to that company.

The Air Force Association also added its support to Junior ROTC, claiming that it "helps provide sound citizenship background and self discipline."[27] The Chamber of Commerce, however, did not support Junior ROTC, because it accepted the Department of Defense' statement that there was no military requirement for the program.

The Veterans of Foreign War added their support, and the Military Order of the World War also backed the program. The latter stated that "there can be no better investment in the youth of our country than that of military training at the impressionistic high school age."[28]

The support of these military organizations contradicts a commonly stated view that militarists themselves would be the least likely to militarize the world. Rather, those who come to believe in military values as a way of life seem to be most anxious to spread that way of life. They were eminently successful in the ROTC Vitalization Act of 1964, and they were as aggressive and well organized as the anti-militarists were in-effective.[29] American educators were conspicuous by their absence. Neither the American Association of University Professors nor the National Education Association (the main national organization of public school educators) even sent a representative, though their offices are in the same city where the hearings were held. And so a rapid expansion of military programs in high schools began in the mid-1960's, nearly doubling from 1964 to 1967, soon to expand nearly fivefold. Soon there will probably be 1200 high schools in the United States that teach militarism, which in-cludes firing rifles at models of the human body and learning to throw hand grenades, as part of their "educational" offering. Until 1966 only the Army had Junior ROTC programs, but beginning in 1966, new programs were started under the Navy and Air Force. Schools need not accept these 1200 programs, but many educators believe in regimentation and in ac-cepting anything that does not come out of the local school budget. Until educators see the difference between education for choice and in-doctrination for conformity, it is not likely that many schools will pass up this warfare state generosity. From 1964 to mid-1969, Jr. ROTC programs rose from 254 to 763. In 1964, 55 programs were mandatory. By 1969, 157 had become mandatory. The militarization of American high schools tripled in five years.

A few programs have been rejected. In one community in Hawaii in 1965, arguments for and against the program were presented. One speaker told parents in brutally honest language — "If you want your children to go to school to learn to kill, vote for the program." The final vote was substantially in opposition. In 1966 the Superintendent of Schools of the State of Hawaii, Lowell Jackson, obtained a change in policy so that the four mandatory high school programs were changed to voluntary programs. If this can be done in a state as militarily influenced as Hawaii, it can be done elsewhere, providing there is educational leadership.

The record of public school educators does not provide many instances which encourage optimism. In spite of the fact that educators often proclaim that they have made substantial contributions toward the development of American freedom, they have more often served the dominant pressures.[30] With the rise of military influence, public schools have usually become supporters of militarism.

OTHER MILITARY INFLUENCES

One of the most dramatic conversions toward military values occurred after the Russians sent up their "sputnik." The response by American centers of power was that we must be "behind", and the schools were assumed to be one of the institutions responsible for our "defeat." Admiral Rickover became a leading exponent of this thesis and therefore, in the public mind, an authority on education. The American high school hero had for many years been either the football star or the young man being groomed for the role of junior executive in American industry. Within a few months the symbolism changed. Academically gifted students, particularly those who seemed gifted in mathematics and physics, were suddenly given the limelight. There were the new math programs and various new science programs, and the public school curriculum shifted in the direction of the physical sciences. Though the social sciences and the humanities are more promising for creating a humane and peaceful world, the schools joined the bandwagon and became producers of human grist for the military-industrial mill.

The combination of military pressures and "cooperative" educators has produced some grotesque results. The Air Force has been particularly enthusiastic about "educating" Americans ever since some American soldiers were considered to have been "brainwashed" by the Chinese Communists during the Korean War. The Air Force would not use the term "brainwashing" with respect to its own processes, for it becomes more patriotic to call it "education" when it is done by the American Armed Forces. An Air Force "education" pamphlet was published in

1960 for the stated purpose of getting public school counselors to "help students maintain ability and the will to fight."[31] It was titled *The Struggle for Men's Minds.*[32] The pamphlet was prefaced by a quotation which included the statement, "Every society has a right to . . . prohibit the propagation of opinions which have a dangerous tendency . . .. No member of society has a right to teach any doctrine contrary to what the society holds to be true."[33] This statement denies the concept of academic freedom, which is based on the democratic concept of free speech translated into teaching as freedom of inquiry and, therefore, freedom to learn.

Teachers often obtained exemption from the draft, a privileged status which may help them feel obligated and less free to be critical of the military. Some teachers and professors are members of military reserves, seduced by extra pay, free air travel, and other subsidies, and they often develop a dependence on military institutions and military values.

COLLEGE ROTC

The military and its devotees have tried for many years to make military values more influential in American schools, and during the periods of war anxiety they have made substantial inroads. The massive ROTC movement, which first began in the Civil War with what is now known both as the Morrill Act and the Land-Grant Act of 1862. This act provided federal land to the states to be used to provide funds for at least one college in each state which was to emphasize agriculture and mechanical arts, but the bill also mandated inclusion of "military tactics."[34]

When the land-grant colleges were created they all offered military courses, at first taught by faculty members who had been in the Army, later by regular Army officers assigned to ROTC programs. World War I gave a stimulus to ROTC, and the National Defense Act of 1916 not only provided greater federal support of college ROTC but also provided funds to establish ROTC at the *high school* level in both public and private schools. The high school military programs were not required by federal law, and schools that wanted them had to make a request. But at the college level, not only were the *programs* required, but the War Department stipulated that two years of ROTC was *to be compulsory for all male students attending land-grant colleges.*

Though most of the colleges docilely accepted these privisions, ferment developed, and both faculty and students began questioning the education legitimacy of ROTC courses. The military programs had dual objectives — both to train soldiers and to *develop citizens.* The military training itself produced student reaction because it was often geared to a level of intelligence insultingly lower than that of the average college student. But reaction was particularly strong with respect to the presumptuous goal of the military in dictating to civilian students the meaning of democratic citizenship. Lyons and Masland describe the conflict between the self-righteous determination of the military and the rising resistance of the college educators as follows:

"For the officer steeped in the traditions of his country as taught at West Point, it was undoubtedly difficult to comprehend that there was a difference between indoctrination and education, between having a code of ethics thrust upon a student and allowing him to develop his own philosophy of living through inquiry and examination."[35]

The military, with its own special values would be difficult for a college to control even if it limited its objectives to military goals. But the military has often wanted to define the civilian world in terms of its own value system. This ethnocentricity is nothing very new in human behavior, but it is something very dangerous to a democracy. For instance, the Training Manual of the American Army in 1928 offered the following remarkable definition of democracy:

"A government of the masses. Authority derived through mass meetings or any other form of 'direct' expression. Results in mobocracy. Attitude toward property is communistic---negating property rights. Attitude toward law is that the will of the majority shall regulate, whether it be based upon deliberation or governed by passion, prejudice, and impulse, without restraint or regard to consequences. Results in demagogism, license, agitation, discontent, anarchy."[36]

As resistance grew in the 1920's against the military's attempt to define the American way of life and against required college ROTC, those who offered resistance were "accused of being manipulated by Bolshevik conspirators if they were not Bolsheviks themselves."[37] And in 1926, when a group called the Committee on Militarism in Education, supported by such eminent educators as John Dewey, tried to develop a bill to abolish compulsory ROTC, a representative of the Reserve Officers Association stated that "the purpose of the bill is entirely in accord with the declared purposes and objectives of every pacifist, defeatist, socialist, and communist organization in the United States."[38]

Nevertheless, those who demanded that ROTC be elective had been making some headway. In 1923 the University of Wisconsin made such a strong demand for an elective program that the state legislature put ROTC on an elective basis. Enrollment dropped precipitously, but the War Department did not challenge the state law. In 1930 the United States Attorney General clarified Wisconsin's action by decreeing that the Morrill Act required only that a course in military tactics be offered but did not obligate colleges to make it a requirement. However, most colleges and organized educational associations were in favor of the compulsory requirement, and it was not until 1933 that a second institution, the University of Minnesota, also changed to an elective program. From then on other colleges became more active, and with a rising movement against militarism in the schools "the mid-1930's could point to seventeen colleges that had dropped ROTC altogether since 1921 and seven that had changed from compulsory to elective.''39

Some of the ROTC programs were suspended during World War II, but they were resumed after the war. By 1969 there were 365 ROTC programs in the United States connected with the Army, Air Force, and Navy. There were 477 programs in 1967 prior to the rising student anti-militarism during the Vietnam war. These programs have always produced varying degrees of conflict with students and faculty, and the central issues have been and continue to be:

1. Compulsory instead of elective ROTC requirements for male students in the majority of colleges with ROTC programs.

2. An educational method stressing training and indoctrination in conflict with the central university commitment toward study and inquiry.

3. Centralized national control of ROTC programs violating the institutional autonomy of colleges and universities.

4. Sub-standard preparation of ROTC instructors (or none at all) in certain ROTC courses such as military history; geography, and international relations.

5. The commitment toward violence and killing instead of a humane ethic.

6. The demands on student time which distract from what is considered legitimate college and university education.

THE COMPULSION ISSUE

1. The compulsory requirements have not been imposed by the federal government since 1930, but many public land-grant colleges still retain their earlier requirement and force all male students to take two years of ROTC. Students from families with sufficient money to attend a private school can be released from these demands — one more example of a long tradition that makes those with money less susceptible to military demands on their life. (Even in the days of the Civil War, the wealthy could buy their way out of the military draft by paying $300.)

But within the last few years students and faculty have become increasingly active, and from 1960 to 1969 they managed to get 270 ROTC programs changed from compulsory to elective status. In 1969, 96 schools remained on the old compulsory status, with every likelihood that more will become voluntary.

Some administrations and regents are still sensitive to incurring possible criticism of the ''patriotism'' and ''Americanism'' of their college. They hesitate to move to a voluntary status, fearing criticism from nationalists, though more freedom of choice would be consistent with some of the central American traditions. Federal law has never required mandatory ROTC and since 1957 the Department of Defense has been entirely indifferent to whether a college required ROTC or made it elective.

Colleges and universities that retain compulsory ROTC are faced with embarrassing questions about their educational aims, even more than the schools which keep ROTC on campus as an elective. An institution that requires a course is, by implication, asserting that the course is so high on the hierarchy of values that it cannot be left to the student's elective choice. Therefore, when ROTC is required in an American university it represents some of the central values of the institution, for the values of an institution are based more pertinently on what it does than on what it says. So, by implication, 96 American ''colleges'' and ''universities'' continued (in 1969) to embrace military values as central characteristics of their higher ''education''.

THE INDOCTRINATION ISSUE

2. The value conflicts between ROTC and the larger university are especially sharp in relation to educational method. Whereas the central method in most American universities is claimed to be critical inquiry, the military is more alanogous to a sub-culture in which an adolescent is inducted into a way of life, and military teaching methods are therefore primarily indoctrinational. So conflict is often strong on campuses between the professors who believe that understanding should be the educational goal, and the ROTC instructors, who believe that obedient performance should be the goal. The professors often distinguish between education and training; the ROTC instructors usually make no distinction. The professors are usually committed to a model of an *open* society of obedience and belief.

Though the military labels itself a ''profession,'' it is qualitatively different from the other professional schools ordinarily connected with higher education. While members of what are ordinarily considered professions have a large measure of autonomy, the military member is encouraged to lose his autonomy and individual identity in order to develop efficient obedience. As Lyons points out, ''the special behavioral pattern which distinguishes the military from other professions is achieved through a rigorous program of self-denial, of almost monastic existence, of obedience to ritual from which there is no recourse and no doubting.''[40] So ROTC is as anomalous on a university campus as a religious order would be, at least with respect to methods of teaching.

To be sure, some university professors see no issue; they seem to accept whatever may be the status quo. Others recognize the conflict in values, yet hold the view of Lyons and Masland that there needs to be an alliance between the professors and the military, presumably for national survival. Lyons and Masland contend that the larger manpower needs of the nation should supersede other considerations. These assumptions were strongly questioned in an article by Allan Brick, who stated:

"Lyons and Masland . . . do not demonstrate the connections which for them exist between that need for survival and an undeviating reliance upon military power. Only by admitting such connections might one agree that the functions of the university might continue to be sacrificed to military training."[41]

In fact Professor Brick argues that survival is more likely if ROTC is entirely removed from the campus, permitting a high quality of education, uncorrupted by militarism. He charges:

"The theoreticians of the armed forces recognize the necessity of rigidifying a boy's mind before he is able to think for himself. They recognize that, left alone, a young man might see for himself whether or not connections exist between survival and reliance on military power, and that, left alone, he might come up with unorthodox answers. They fear . . . nonmilitary solutions to international problems. They fear the thinking of college graduates whose minds were not formed by military methods."[42]

THE AUTONOMY ISSUE

3. Federal control of American education has long been a fear of those who have resisted federal financial aid. Yet it has seldom been pointed out that ROTC represented an already established instance of the most extreme and insidious control of education that one could reasonably expect in American society. ROTC is not merely federally controlled, but militarily controlled. It includes an almost entirely prescribed curriculum, centrally controlled by the Pentagon and taught by instructors who are controlled by the Pentagon. It is analogous to a condition where all professional schools of education would be controlled by the U.S. Office of Education, with a prescribed curriculum, and with instructors in colleges of education who would be members of the U.S. Office of Education for purposes of retention, promotion, and salary.

Even this analogy, using teacher education, does not sufficiently illuminate the corruption of university autonomy involved in ROTC programs, for a U.S. Office of Education would probably share many of the values in relation to teaching methods and educational goals which are found in higher education. But ROTC clashes fundamentally in relation to both methods and objectives, for Pentagon leadership has an outlook far removed from the traditions of higher education.

It is true that the normal professions represented on a campus (such as law, medicine, pharmacy, engineering, and teacher education) have organizations which influence standards and even university accreditation. But the standards are typically general, flexible, and subject to influence by a particular university which wishes to have room for innovation. Lyons points out:

"In contrast, a proposal by Harvard University in 1955 to adjust the Army ROTC program to take better advantage of the kind of education the university had to offer was turned down by the Department of the Army on the argument . . . that any modification had to be thought of in terms of its eventual extension to other institutions."[43]

Harvard at least had the legal choice of retaining or excluding military courses. But land-grant institutions, until the Morrill Act is changed, at the present time must at least offer a course in "military tactics." However they are under no obligation to offer ROTC courses to meet the requirement.

The structure of academic freedom, central to the general ethical-professional commitment of college faculty, is undercut by the existence of ROTC. Regular college faculty are organized to provide encouragment and defense of other faculty who use their academic freedom within the framework of their academic competence. ROTC faculty fall flagrantly outside the entire academic freedom-responsibility standards through their use of indoctrination and non-intellectual subject matter. But the faculty organizations, such as the American Association of University Professors, have no direct disciplining power over instructors in the ROTC, since they exist, as Lyons says, similar to "foreign embassies within otherwise sovereign territories."[44] It is not merely the individual ROTC instructor but the entire ROTC program that violates the AAUP commitments. The AAUP must share the responsibility for having failed to face the issue directly and forcefully. In the meantime, higher education in land-grant colleges lives in a state of unholy alliance.

THE COMPETENCE ISSUE

4. ROTC instructors are often incompetent teachers, according to the ostensible standards of higher education. Most ROTC instruction is predicated on a naive type of philosophical realism, where external demands and information are to be transmitted and learned through stimulus-response conditioning. College teachers generally call this training but not teaching, to the consternation of ROTC instructors, who usually argue that they themselves are officers, therefore leaders, therefore teachers. They point out that they are quite willing to have students question, but they do not mean question the justification of an order or examine goals and purposes. Rather the military is only willing to have soldiers question the efficiency of particular processes of implementation or to clarify understanding of information and orders. It is precisely this closed system of goals and values which conflicts with university objectives.[45] I: represents the way in which a university instructor might be forced to behave if he were under the control of a totalitarian government. Such behavior in an American university is a violation of open inquiry, a

distinguishing feature of a university in a free society, and it conflicts with this most important value of higher education.

ROTC instructors are usually not qualified to teach history, geography, or international politics, yet they attempt to teach such courses, often to students who have been compelled to take ROTC. The Air Force ROTC has shown some recognition of the problem and has shifted more of its courses over to civilian faculty instruction. But Army ROTC continues to hire unqualified instructors. Thirty hours of instruction are required in "American military history," yet the instructors are seldom trained historians, not even trained military historians. They may or may not have *any* background in social sciences except for undergraduate general education requirements. If they studied at West Point they probably focused on science and mechanics. West Point has previously ignored many of the elements of education which are necessary for responsible leadership in the modern world. Though attempts have been made in the latter 1960's to correct some of the deficiencies. In 1962, when David Boroff made a study of West Point, he found that the social sciences and humanities were deemphasized and a standard social science course such as anthropology was not even offered. West Point instructors usually had minimum preparation in whatever courses they offered, but there were fewer Ph.D's on the teaching staff than there are at the better junior colleges. The majority of instructors had no more than a bachelor's degree, often from another military school.[46] Boroff found even their conception of the military to be seriously deficient. He said, "I was startled at the pre-nuclear consciousness of both officers and cadets. There seemed to be a striking failure to recognize that warfare has entered a radically new phase with the introduction of nuclear weapons."[47]

By 1969 the weakness in academic preparation of faculty continued, with only six percent of the faculty holding doctorates. But there had been a substantial addition to the social science curriculum, even though the curriculum continued to focus on science and mechanics.[48]

Army ROTC instructors not only teach military history, they also teach "The Role of the United States in World Affairs." The mispreparation of the instructor, with a possible B.S. in electrical engineering, often makes this course an academic catastrophe. In an interview with personnel at one Army ROTC unit, the writer was told that "they do teach about Communism, to get the students to hate it." The ROTC instructors admitted that none of them were qualified to teach this course. They admitted that they indoctrinated students with their own beliefs; as justification, they offered that their beliefs were based on American mores. They *thought* they were acting consistently with the purposes of a university. As one officer commented, "A university would not want extreme views — only accepted beliefs." The others agreed.

ROTC instructors use required materials prepared by the Pentagon, ordinarily with no indication of authorship. The history book used in Army

ROTC is titled *American History, 1607-1958.*[49] It was in fact written by twelve men with normal academic qualifications, and the book is superior to most military texts, though the military history is not treated contextually and therefore gives one little understanding of its relation to social, political, or cultural events. However, another text, the *Role of the United States in World Affairs* text is conspicuously value-loaded to serve the military outlook. Published in 1960, it says, "International conflict is an inevitable feature of world politics." It further states, "The United States is essentially a Christian nation"[50] and "it is certain that the enduring aspiration sought by the leaders of the Soviet Communist State is the *establishment of universal Soviet communism throughout the world, dominated by the U.S.S.R.*"[51] (italics mine). Though this official government publication was printed in 1960, four years after the Soviet Union affirmed a policy of co-existence with the west, the text was retained for use in ROTC programs. It states, "No amount of study and analysis of conditions in the Soviet Union can discover or substantiate any evidence of the modification of the ultimate purpose of Soviet communism, *the elimination of capitalism and capitalistic states, and the achievements of Communist world domination, with universal headquarters in Moscow.*" (Italics mine)

The book divides the world into the "Communist world" and the "free world," the latter including fascist military dictatorships. It is admitted that some of the "free world" nations are not democratic, but they are accepted if they are anti-communistic. Dictatorships such as Spain, Portugal, Taiwan, and many Latin American countries are considered allies, partially because they are anti-communistic but especially because they provide American military bases. Though Taiwan is recognized as a dictatorship, it is still in the "free world," and it is seen to be capable of becoming "more and more democratic."[52] However, there is no indication that it would be possible for either Russia or Communist China to become similarly transformed.

The term "power" is used in this book only to denote military and economic power, a rather ironic "American" point of view considering that the Communists are often the ones who are accused of a materialistic outlook. For instance, any possibility for "victory" is said to be based on science and technology: "when two great associations of national power become stalemated in their scientific research and technological development, the first to establish a significant scientific breakthrough may achieve victory by that margin."[53]

American economic wealth is described in terms of gross national product, and the superiority of Americans is implied throughout in a lauditory and ethnocentric comparative treatment of American society. Nothing is mentioned about the range in the distribution of wealth in the United States — the amount of poverty, nor the flagrant civil liberties issues. Yet this book has been given to college students as an official statement of the "role of the United States in world affairs." It is little more than an anti-communist propaganda tract. It is because of such materials that the more sophisticated college students have considered ROTC courses to be absurd. The less sophisticated students have often accepted this material as the truth.

By 1970 a new manual titled *World Change And Military Implications* had replaced the older text, and the new text suggests the offical ideological emphasis for the 1970's. It carries a somewhat more concilliatory tone and speaks favorably of *multilateral* coordination of aid programs. It continues to define the future in terms of nation-states, but even though it takes no account of a possible supra-national system of peace keeping it says that it is "imperative for the United States to conduct serious negotiations for international agreement on limitation, reduction, and control of armaments." [54] Seldom are the peace keeping requirements of the nuclear era given recognition in military programs and it is encouraging to finally see a break-through.

However, other sections of the manual continues to define the world in terms of the Communist bloc and the free world.[55] The professional soldier is encouraged to think of himself as an instrument of nation building, which excludes revolutionary change in government especially by communist revolutionaries. The role of the American military is to increasingly "defeat insurgency" and to stabilize existing governments.[56] America is to continue to be on the side of economic development and the political status quo, as though the only lesson in Vietnam has been to improve the techniques for achieving the *same* foreign policy goals.

The ROTC instructor has seldom been sufficiently competent to aid students in being intelligently critical of military materials. His assigned role is to indoctrinate rather than to understand. Universities support a different *standard* of competence by which the ROTC instructor is considered a propagandist in conflict with official university standards of critical inquiry.

THE COMMITMENT TO VIOLENCE ISSUE

5. Higher education in the United States has been based on both intellectual and humanistic traditions, and thus has encouraged the college student to become a morally sensitive and responsive person through studies in the humanities. He may learn to develop his own esthetic and moral feelings through music, art, literature, religion, philosophy, or drama. All this is normal to the purposes of higher education. But when an agency attached to a university specializes in teaching young men how to kill, an understandable conflict and revulsion occurs. Instruction in violence is hardly admired, and there often is so little common outlook between ROTC faculty and the humanistically oriented faculty that there may be little basis even for communication. This does not mean that faculty who object to the existence of specialists in violence on a campus

necessarily oppose the idea of having armed forces in modern society. Quite the opposite, they often consider such men necessary to a non-internationally organized world — and even necessary as a police force in an internationally organized world. The objection is that the university should be perverted by offering such training. To see young men on a university campus going to their next "class," a firing line where they shoot at mock-ups of human beings, is as hideously inconsistent with the humanistic purposes of higher education as it would be to have a course such as Execution 101. An increased involvement by higher education in resolving current conflicts and aiding in constructive development by no means necessitates courses in learning to wage war.

Another view supporting ROTC is that the university is merely a creature of the state, with no supranational moral commitment. This view embraces some of the central assumptions of political totalitarianism. It assumes that human "needs" are whatever a government says they are. Virtually any demand can therefore be made on higher education if it is said to serve national "interests." Here are shades of the theory of the corporate state, where all the sub-units feed into the mythical larger state, and where an efficient contribution to a uncritically accepted conception of the "common good" is the rationale of correct individual and institutional behavior.

There is also the similar view that higher education is, as Robert Hutchins used to say, for hire. This view has recently been propounded as the conception of the "multiversity," where instead of its having a moral-intellectual commitment to mankind, the university is in the service of the national government or any other agency that can pay for its services. This conception makes higher education similar to the world's oldest "profession" — the servant of the highest bidder.

Finally there is the view that ROTC should be used to build the *character* of American youth. This view usually plays down the commitment to violence and killing that is central to military purposes. and plays up the values of drill, command, and service. Senator Russell of Georgia, in helping pass the ROTC Vitalization Act of 1964, argued that ROTC is not merely necessary for military reasons, but *morally* good.[57] ROTC departments advertise their programs with similar claims. Such totalitarian concepts of higher education accommodate the "ethical" commitment of ROTC to violence. But the goals of inquiry and the dedication to a humane ethic in higher education conflict with military programs on college campuses.

THE WASTE OF TIME ISSUE

6. With the increasing pressures on college students to understand a complicated world, the remaining compulsory ROTC programs place a demand during the first two years which creates a special burden for male students. Many find it difficult to keep up with the normal college

requirements, and many work part-time to meet expenses. Army ROTC requires a minimum of three hours a week during the first two years, and for those who stay in the program, five hours a week during the last two years.

Students question the value of some of the training even for military purposes, for much of it consists of what is euphemistically called "leadership laboratory," which is mostly *drill.* Typically the students in the required first two years are drilled by those who have voluntarily stayed through the third and fourth years.

Even educators who favor the idea of ROTC often agree that the usual programs are largely a waste of time. Lyons and Masland say the Army ROTC curriculum "is concerned too much with details that are easily forgotten, and too frequently fails to challenge the imagination of the superior student, or even in many cases, of the average student."[58] They suggest that military leadership should be based on educational concepts similar to those of law and medicine, which include a heavy emphasis on pre-professional education followed by induction in the specializations of the profession. This would include deferment of specialized instruction until the graduate period, while liberal-general education and broad general principles relating to the profession would be taught at the undergraduate level.

There appears to be a direct correlation between the academic quality of an institution and its aversion to ROTC. About *60 percent* of the students are usually lost when ROTC first becomes voluntary. When the University of Oregon converted to a voluntary ROTC, it lost about 75 percent. The University of California lost 81 *percent,* and Harvard's voluntary program had nearly 90 *percent* of its undergraduates avoiding ROTC.

According to one study, students avoid ROTC primarily because of the "time involved" and "disinterest in the content."[59] As the demands become more extensive and the subject matter more complicated in the regular college curriculum, the infringement on the student's time is likely to be felt even more acutely. And so some students and faculty oppose ROTC, not on moral or ethical grounds but simply because it is a waste of time.

Rising anti-militarism, aided by the Vietnam war, has given the critics of ROTC programs enough power on American campuses to force a retreat of ROTC programs. A strong trend developed in the later 60's to make ROTC voluntary in land grant institutions and to abolish the programs in many private institutions. Even where programs are retained they are increasingly being stripped of academic credit. The Pentagon, fearing that a retreat might grow into a rout, has given more power to local campus ROTC directors to negotiate a program acceptable to the university. As a result, ROTC courses requiring academic competence are beginning to be shifted into academic departments and the Pentagon is being faced with a rebellion which may not easily yield to its techniques of counter-insurgency.[60]

THE MILITARY-INDUSTRIAL-UNIVERSITY COMPLEX

Since World War II, the technology of military systems has become increasingly complex, and Pentagon interests have included not only the "hardware" of weapons research but also the "software" research of the social sciences, often used to help subvert left wing revolutionary movements in other nations. University professors in the applied, natural, and social sciences have been coveted by the Department of Defense, for their research has been a vital link in the military-industrial complex. The war system requires cooperation between government, industry, and the universities, and from the 1940's to the later 1960's the alliance was unshaken.

At first, the universities assumed that they could retain independence from the Pentagon even while serving it. By the end of the 1960's, this naive myth was less widely shared, but the universities were so enmeshed in Pentagon influence that deescalation of influence was not easy. And, as with the war in Vietnam, not everyone wanted to deescalate.

By 1969 the Pentagon had 5,000 contracts with university scientists, and each contract usually supported other faculty and graduate assistants. Ten universities received over 40 percent of the entire Pentagon research budget, while the remainder was spread between "think tanks" and other universities. The "think tanks," such as the Stanford Research Institute have often been only nominally separated from the universities for university faculty usually work in both institutions. In 1968 the top ten universities and their annual D.O.D. funds were:

M.I.T.	$119,100,000
John Hopkins	57,600,000
University of California	17,300,000
Stanford	16,400,000
University of Rochester	13,100,000
Cornell	12,500,000
Illinois Institute of Tech.	12,100,000
Penn. State	10,500,000
Columbia	9,900,000
University of Michigan	9,400,000

These are not merely state universities, but also the so called "private" universities. Harvard, Princeton, and Cal. Tech. have been highly involved in Pentagon research. About 10 times as many professors have requested D.O.D. funds as have received them. Clearly many professors manage to adjust their alleged disinterested pursuit of truth so that their interests coincide with the sources of funds. In that sense, the professors corrupt themselves by their own prostitution. But prostitution is also a matter of supply and demand. If there were more sources of research funds, the universities could choose between patrons. The D.O.D. is the most wealthy patron of research funds and the payer of the piper usually calls the tunes.

Many professors do not believe they are prostituting themselves or the university to work for the D.O.D. Many think of themselves mainly as nationalists, and if they have pre-atomic conceptions of national defense, they consider the work a contribution to their society. The professor is often a high level technician, not broadly educated, who is politically still a part of the Reader's Digest culture.

In the latter 1960's there has been, however, a dawning awareness that the Pentagon's goals have closer relationship to annihilation than to survival and that the university has been undermining itself by contributing to the destruction of life instead of to its preservation and development. The use of the secrecy required in many military contracts has been particularly a target of criticism.

The secret contract is the most universally rejected, but contracts to undertake research involving classified research are usually not secret. Harvard was the first to reject all institutional classified research. John Hopkins has followed and other universities have been either considering cutting down on classified projects or on eliminating them all together. Their claims are somewhat deceptive, however, for they often mean that they are abandoning classified publication of results while continuing to use classified sources.

Even though Harvard has abandoned institutional classified research, the faculty has not. A distinction is made between an individual faculty contract and a university project. There is no binding professional ethic among university professors that forbids working on secret war projects, and so an immense amount of work is done on that basis.

Academic freedom, in this context, is in effect, the freedom to undermine the principle of an intellectually open society, for the scientific process that is claimed to underlie university research is undermined either by restriction on the availability of research findings or restriction on access to information. Science requires open cross verification of sources, but the American professor has a long way to go to show that he has given his loyalty more to the open society of science than to the closed society of national military systems.

As a consequence, it continues to be normal for most universities to contract for research that uses classified material and therefore requires the use of a security officer on campus and D.O.D. procedures for restricting documents to students and faculty who have security clearances. Faculty who have security clearance access to classified material, or who continue to keep their research findings secret to anyone outside the Pentagon political system contribute to the corruption of the transnational meaning of a university and reinforce the ethics of totalitarian systems. Paul Goodman has called this process "the republic of science," illuminating the contradiction between political elitism and the open public verification necessary to science. Science, being open, is "democratic."

The universities have begun to extricate themselves from the war game but they still have a long way to go. The protests of students, the expose's of journalists (like Seymour Hersh on *Chemical Biological Warfare*) and muckraking journals such as *Ramparts* have been useful prods to the complacency of university establishments. The university is a vital link in Pentagon power, and while campuses may appear to be centers of vociferous war protest, many professors are carrying on their war complicity.

Michigan State University professors helped establish American interventionism in Vietnam, and the CIA has financed a great variety of university projects, even student organizations. James Ridgeway says the universities war research facilities are arranged in a hierarchy with the University of California's Radiation Laboratory at the top. MIT and John Hopkins design missiles, Cornell designs bombs for Vietnam, Princeton breaks codes for the CIA, and Michigan works on photo reconnaissance and counterinsurgency. Pennsylvania and fifty other universities have been working in chemical, germ, and biological warfare, Princeton works on defoliation, and the University of Pittsburgh has designed new gun sights and better ways of using river and beach mines.[61] Ridgeway concludes that "the universities were bought by the Pentagon long ago."[62]

The interdependency of the university and Defense Department has not been confined to swapping research brains for money, it has also produced an increased migration of faculty into the military-industrial complex and back into the university. Secretary McNamara's systems analyst became chancellor of the University of California.

The government and the war industries also rely on university students for new manpower, and until the Vietnam war revealed the horrors of the war system there was no resistance to the use of campuses as recruitment agencies. Then recruitment by the CIA, by the Armed Forces, and by napalm manufacturers such as Dow Chemical, was protested and even forceably resisted, mainly by students. The typical establishment position, usually supported by the faculty, has been procedural—that the university should have an "open campus," assuming that all employment opportunity is a legitimate function of a university. When students have forcibly blocked recruiters, they have often been arrested or bloodied and maimed by police clubs. What seems to have happened is that the university has been bought and sold for so many purposes that it no longer has a distinguishable "legitimate function." If the university were an intellectual center responsible to all men for the improvement of life, it could then consider itself an "open campus" for ideas and evidence. But it has no obligation to be "open" to military *recruitment*. When Dow, the CIA, and the Marines have been asked to participate in intellectual discussions, they usually have refused. The university has no more obligation to be open to recruitment by the Marines than by the Mafia, but they should uphold the right, even the opportunity, for both of them to present their respective views on the need for violence or whatever other topic they may wish to discuss in an open forum.[63]

THE MYTH OF OBJECTIVITY

Though a slow awakening is developing in American universities, the old myths about objectivity and neutrality still predominate. The most common standard of objectivity is the use of *quantifiable* scientific research. If the research on defoliation of tropical vegetation meets the requisite research standards it is "objective," no matter who starves when the Pentagon uses the research to implement American foreign policy. Faculty often fail to realize that knowledge is a form of power, and that it is usually used within particular social and political systems. When faculty strengthen a war-system they are part of that system. They are also part of the system when they feign neutrality, for their indifference only reinforces existing systems, though not as much as a direct contribution. To deny partisanship does not make the faculty member neutral, it only makes him naive.

The selection of one research problem rather than another tends to predetermine the probable social consequences. We cannot always control the use of knowledge but we can select the kind of projects that are most needed to improve human life and we can be open about the values we try to affirm. And we can refuse to cooperate with some segments of the human race who are likely to destroy others to serve their own ends.

The university has been a vital link in preserving the war system, for modern war systems are highly technical and they require the advanced research that is most available in universities. As faculties become agents of death and subversion, they corrupt themselves while they perpetuate an anachronistic system of "defense" that is little more than a cancer on the human race. If universities could transfer their "defense" efforts into the problems of the development of better systems of international law, peace keeping, and economic development, they could really contribute to human welfare and to genuine national and international defense.

ANNIHILATION BY DEFAULT

Aside from the direct war contribution of many American schools, the very irrelevance of virtually all American education to human survival demands consideration. The parading of nationalistic symbols such as songs and salutes diminishes at the college level, but seldom do students at any level study anything relevant to the elimination of thermonuclear war. Courses usually ignore the central problems of our age. Courses that are problem-centered are seldom rigorous, and they usually omit non-

112

conventional views, particularly below the college level. Curriculum trends during the latter 1950's and 60's emphasized subject-centered curriculum. Math and science, followed gradually by other subject areas, have been carefully pre-packaged by university scholars for use in elementary schools and high schools. The professors who package these subjects are often out of contact with those who work in other fields, and many are out of touch with the problems of the larger world, such as war prevention in the atomic age. So though the new curriculum has reduced the lag with university subjects and has provided more logical organization of subjects, it has the defect of compartmentalization. It is atomistic rather than integrative. It is more consistent with the intellecutal life within the modern university, but it is as far removed as ever from the vital issues of the larger society.

Though college faculty have been more active in anti-war movements than most groups, they seldom direct their research or their teaching toward the study of war prevention. Schools at all levels are so often out of touch with both the experience of students and the vital issues of our time that those young people who are anxious to obtain the kind of knowledge which gives them a basis for understanding and participating in vital contemporary issues usually find institutional education to be trivial and irrelevant. If they have a strong sense of life and want knowledge to be active and important, schooling is often a tedious bore. They don't fail their classes; their classes too often fail them. Not all young people are purposeful, and the schools are often able to transform the more amorphous students according to its own mechanical and prosaic pattern. They often form people who are as dull and prosaic as the schools. Most graduates obediently and uncritically fit into other equally dehumanizing institutions and become conventional models of ''success.'' This is the normal route for becoming a respectable citizen.

Some students survive institutional education by playing the game. They hold a cynical view toward the system and offer only surface conformity while personally judging the system to be hypocritical and superficial. While playing the game they concentrate on peripheral activities for their real education. They form political action groups, demonstrations, community action projects, and independent study projects. This becomes their real education. Some get started before college, but most of this kind of involvement with the real world begins at the college level — not because of, but in spite of, the educational system. There are exceptional schools and exceptional teachers, but the vast majority of American schools are archaic.

The Vietnam war has sparked some political concern, but the majority of professors have continued to be fixated on respectability, fiddling while the nuclear world prepares to burn.[64] Theodore Roszak has made an even stronger indictment:

Until the recent rash of campus protest related to the Vietnam war, nothing has so characterized the American academic as a condition of entrenched social irrelevance, so highly developed that it would be comic if it were not sufficiently serious in its implications to stand condemned as an act of criminal deliquency.[65]

Schools are not the only institutions that have retained pre-atomic thinking in a post-atomic world. Virtually all American institutions have kept the old structures and the old assumptions. Modern Americans rely on expanding technology for their salvation. Industry creates a plethora of new products, the military continuously designs new weapons, and the schools turn to teaching machines, computers, and other electronic equipment to solve the problems of learning. Rarely is there any broad social planning that combines human needs with technical means. The response to each new crisis is seen primarily as a demand for new technology; we do what is technologically possible not what is socially desirable and ecologically imperative. The central force in the society is to make money, whether or not the production serves the larger needs of survival and social justice. The result is an ecologically imbalanced, ad-hoc, atomistic, non-integrated society working best for those who have wealth, but in fact threatening the future of everyone.

The schools have been part of the old politics, reinforcing the old systems by keeping students ignorant of the vital issues of our age. For the schools, too, it is the end of an era. They must either begin to help students learn to participate in the reconstruction of the old systems or they will continue to keep the society locked into its pre-atomic reverie, opting for annihilation.

PART III

RECONSTRUCTING AMERICAN SOCIETY

CHAPTER VI

EDUCATION FOR SURVIVAL

The previous chapters have tried to describe ways in which militarism, one of the most obsolete and pathological aspects of American culture, continues to perpetuate its institutions and its ideology. The book is based on the premise that when people are taught to become cultural agents in the perpetuation of fundamentally obsolete institutions, they threaten the future of society. When people lack a global perspective, they can only evaluate the adequacy of sub-units such as nations or military institutions through the value system of those same sub-units. But since each system tends to create its own justifying values, it becomes difficult for people to transform their own institutions. People usually become psychologically locked into subsystems.

Our institutions vary in their degree of obsolesence. Americans typically say that an institution is adequate because it "works". But it may "work" in some limited, short range sense, and yet not work in a broader, long range sense. Educating for survival requires that more integral and long range assessments be made. It requires that we have some theory of relevance, some standard by which to measure institutions and habits, and it requires that we assess our social habits on the basis of the alternative ways in which we might be using our time and our energy.

Ironically, one of the major obstacles to survival in the United States is the American conception of ''freedom.'' Each national and cultural system creates its own meaning of freedom. Typically Americans offer their meaning as the universally correct meaning, without being aware of the particular historical context in which such beliefs developed. Most Americans not only proclaim themselves ''free'' but they usually assume that they are the legitimate authority to define the true meaning of freedom for all men.

The dominant conception of freedom in American society is that people should be free *from* restriction, ie. free to do what they want to do. This negative freedom, combined with the ideology of individualism, contributes to a hedonistic social ethic and an anarchistic social, political, and economic structure. These particular notions of freedom, whatever their historical relationship to the frontier, Protestantism, and laissez faire economics, are now a hindrance not only to survival but also to choosing the kind of future we really want. For the freedom to survive and have a better world requires cooperative social planning.

The ideology of individual freedom has encouraged political indifference and elitist decision-making systems. Some have been more free than others to decide policy, and they have made the decisions which have circumscribed the freedom of the majority. This decision making elite has sometimes gained its power by consent but often by usurpation of special privilege. Systems that perpetuate the mal-distribution of power produce mal-distributions of wealth and require re-planning in order to achieve more social justice. But social planning at a national and international level is now needed not merely to provide more justice to the underprivileged but also to provide survival for the privileged. Planning now has more chance of succeeding than ever before, because neither the rich nor the poor can long survive without fundamental change. Nuclear war and pollution are no respecters of the rich. For many young people the "do your own thing" ethic may indicate a positive thrust toward individual integrity in the face of an overly organized and manipulative society. "Do your own thing" is merely a romantic echo of the individualism of the American past. We now work for survival together or we perish together.

Until the twentieth century, people have lacked the knowledge necessary for basic replanning, for they did not have the social science tools necessary to understand their values and they lacked the capacity to predict and control social change. Knowledge in these areas is still quite limited, but it does permit us to examine and create possible futures that we were previously unable to do. We no longer need to be tied to old habits, but by and large we still are, for the new knowledge is not adequately shared. Widespread ignorance is the main basis for the relative inflexibility of most contemporary institutions.

The old education was mainly education for individual economic success. The new education for survival and social progress must be aimed at developing integrated social planning and must be based on an ecological understanding of the world. Such education can be taught within schools, but mass media are probably even more influential. The new education needs to become part of the normal social experience of living and working within the society.

The power to choose and participate in change opens up enormously hopeful possibilities for the meaning of life, and therefore calls for urgent application as a social method. Man's technological capacity for cataclysmic destruction is now organized within antiquated pre-atomic political systems in which nation-states continue to threaten each other and plan to carry out their threats even if most or all of the human race is destroyed in the process. As Kenneth Boulding has said, "If the human race is to survive it will have to change its ways of thinking more in the next 25 years than in the last 25,000." While we continue to be part of a national political system, (and more and more young people are opting out) we must first effect change within the institutions over which we have most control. So while Americans may have suggestions for how the Russians and the Chinese ought to behave, the place for Americans to begin reform is here in the United States. No single country effects international reality more than the United States, and to suggest that there is room for improvement in American national and international behavior would be the understatement of the nuclear era.

America is not a nation of evil people, it is a nation of largely well intentioned people who produce considerable evil by conscientiously doing the wrong thing. Obsolescence is endemic in America because of the inertia of institutional structures and past habits. It isn't that the technology of the petroleum fuel automobile needs improving — the petroleum fuel automobile is obsolete as a mode of transportation. It isn't that the economy needs to be stimulated by creating new goods and new markets — a profit making economy that creates needs, devours resources, maldistributes wealth, and commits ecocide is itself obsolete. It isn't that the draft needs to be eliminated and arms stabilization needs to be established — it is *the war system based on national autonomy* which is obsolete.

Basic systems change is needed, and ignorance of systems alternatives is the major element in keeping the old order intact. The needed social change requires two central elements — one is the ideas and the visions of new futures, which is educational. The other is systems substitution, which is political. *People will prefer the security of the old way unless they can gain security by moving from one system to another.* Therefore reduced military expenditure that creates unemployment without providing new jobs is bad planning. Unilateral disarmament without the creation of a global peace keeping system is bad planning. Urban renewal of old cities without the creation of new cities with built in employment is bad planning.

Culture (social ecology) is too organic to permit planned discontinuity. Lack of transition planning makes people conservative, for it is better to grasp the unsatisfactory certainty of the present than to be cast adrift by unplanned change. The history of social change has been largely the intrusion of outside forces such as weather, disease, famine and war; or inside forces such as technology and population expansion. People have been *reactive* rather than *anticipatory*. But we can now go beyond even the prediction of the future by *creating the future*. People can learn to design the future both nationally and globally, making change intentional and predictable. Such a future can integrate man as a species and manage the planet as a biosphere. But if only an elite group learns to plan, the techniques can be used to exploit and control others. That is why education must not only be universal but based on the objective of learning how to plan.

Planning needs to include understanding of the ways in which political sub-units (nations) have been made obsolete by technological development and population expansion, resulting in a choice of producing global integration or global destruction through war and ecocide. Survival requires a more vigorous and visionary education than has ever existed. If conventional schools cannot perform the job, they must be abandoned. To do the job they must be drastically reformed. There is nothing in human potentiality that prevents this great transition, but the transition is now restricted by the way mis-education in the name of education prevents the development of needed human potentiality by retaining the tunnel vision of the past.

The problem even with what is called revolution is that it is usually not revolutionary enough. By using violence to change government, it is easy to presume that necessary change has occurred. Most revolutionaries are still too much a part of the old order. They are usually pre-atomic and often pre-ecological. Some who have ecological concerns prefer a "greening of America" conception which keeps the old unilateral individualism intact and prevents planned economic, political, and legal systems-change. What is now needed is a revolutionary process in which people collectively design new common ways of life, in which economics becomes a tool to achieve new social and environmental futures rather than an end in itself. Such an education would require that students learn to design social and evironmental futures first at a local level, moving outward until they can consider world futures.

The old order gives priority to economics with secondary consideration to social justice and environmental quality. The shift in these priorities requires a 180 degree transformation, and it provides a basis for an education for survival. It would initiate a cultural revolution which would be more fundamental than the "cultural revolution" of the People's Republic of China, since that revolution was not ecologically based nor global in its outlook. Marxist theory identifies the inherent outcomes of market capitalism but it fails to identify the inherent outcomes of an atomic based nation-state system of international conflict management. It is as naive for the Marxists to believe that armed nation states can live in an anarchistic world in peaceful coexistence as it is for conservatives and liberals to believe that there can be peace when there is mal-distribution of wealth.

PROBABILITY OF WORLD WAR III

A highway system permits prediction with some accuracy not only of the probable annual death rate on the highway but even the probable number of deaths on a particular holiday. Before the highway is built you cannot accurately predict the number who will be killed, but you can be virtually certain that death will occur. Transportation systems, economic systems, military defense systems — have success-failure probabilities built into them. Some transportation systems would greatly increase or reduce deaths, some economic systems greatly raise or lower the probability of business cycles and depressions, some systems of national defense greatly increase or lower the probability of human death. Two things are necessary to predict the outcome — an analysis of the probabilities built into the

119

structure of the system and experience with the system. We have met both requirements with highway transportation systems. We know what to expect of them with respect to human fatality. We also have extensive experience with war systems. We know what to expect of them — they will produce war. But we don't know exactly when or where war will occur.

In the pre-atomic world, international conflict was often both exacerbated and resolved by war systems. Because no adequate international peace-keeping system was developed, the twentieth century has had many minor wars and two major world wars, the latter taking 50 million lives. The pre World War II conception of defense continued after the war. But these nation-state threat systems increased their destructive capacity at an exponential rate. It is typically claimed that we have not had World War III *because* of our nuclear threat system. This ignorance about the nature of the system is comparable to building a new highway and if no one was killed in the first week of use to proclaim that the highway was the cause of the longevity of the citizens of that state. The following week 30 people might be killed, but the basic difference between the highway and nuclear defense systems is that there will never be a time when everyone is on the highway and when virtually everyone is killed. Nation-state nuclear "defense" systems will produce two extremes — either the deceptive feeling of safety when there is no war, or else incomprehensible levels of catastrophe when war occurs. But war doesn't occur because of outside forces or laws of nature — it occurs because particular military and political systems make it inevitable. The question is not whether, but only when and where.

The mutual-deterrence mutual-annihilation system on which present national defense is based is estimated to have between a 1 percent and a 10 percent per year *probability* of system failure. The estimates vary, depending on the analyst, but the most optimistic (1 percent) and the least optimistic (10 percent) give us some sense of the estimated fixed dangers *built into such a system.* 1 And this permits us to compare the danger-safety probabilities of other political systems.

This analysis of alternative *political* systems is virtually never used in national defense planning. A national system of national defense is the only system seriously considered. When the Department of Defense talks about "systems" they are talking about the various kinds of *weapons systems* that might be incorporated into our *traditional political* system of national defense. The myopic commitment to the old political system results in the perpetual technological expansion of the American military system. Research and Development is not research into alternative political structures but into new technological possibilities within the old political system. It can become peace research instead of war research when it examines not only the technical development possibilities but also the political alternatives.

There are a great variety of political alternatives. The world can be radically decentralized into individual nations, each with its own armament and its shifting alliances. It can be organized into regional mutual security units. The dominant pattern in the 50's and 60's has been ''protracted conflict'' by which the two super-powers threaten each other with nuclear deterrence-annihilation. Another pattern that could develop is for the United States and Russia to join together in a military domination of the world. An alliance of advanced nations and another alliance of underdeveloped nations is also an open possibility. All of these structures require war systems which in the present age would very likely be nuclearized. As long as the world is politically fragmented, some form of western 6-gun, self help will be inevitable. There would by more sanity in regional multilateral systems, such as a regionally organized Europe and a regionally organized Africa than there is in autonomous nation-state systems of national defense, but this form of political organization still does not meet the defense requirements of the atomic age, for military threat systems would still be the basis for defense. The number of units in a regionally organized world would be less, reducing the number of variables and the amount of unpredictability. But in all previously described models, aggression or accidental systems failure would mean mutual annihilation and possibly global annihilation.

As yet, we have failed to recognize that *war-systems in the nuclear age no longer provide national security.* They sometimes served as effective systems of defense in the prenuclear era, but there is no longer any defense against nuclear, chemical, or biological weapons carried by intercontinental ballistic missiles. Such systems are primarily *offensive.* Nations must be *willing* to use them in order for them to have credibility, but their use is suicidal. Only a locked-in, one dimensional, habit-madness keeps the old system intact.

AN INTERNATIONAL SYSTEM OF NATIONAL DEFENSE

Order can be maintained *within* a country through minimum violence if people have respect for the laws and the legal processes. The same preconditions are applicable on a global level. For instance, if the United Nations Charter were revised so it represented the people of every country according to population, and if it included a permanent police force, and if in the process of reconstructing UN power there was a period of phased, incremental, simultaneous disarmanent of nations, the structure of an international system for defending nations would be in operation. The Clark-Sohn proposal for *World Peace Through World Law* is a carefully detailed proposal similar to the previous outline.[2]

The goal of ''peace'' is not the same as the goal of a world without war. Peace suggests amiability, tranquility, brotherhood, the lion lying down with the lamb. Or to the Marxist it means the elimination of systems that sustain social-economic class. The many ideological meanings that adhere to the word ''peace'' prevent it from producing an agreement on

121

goals. A world without war is different. It may be a world *with* considerable conflict, therefore not peaceful. But a system of conflict *management* can greatly reduce the chances of war, and in a disarmed world the consequences of war are minimized.

Nations need *military* systems to wage war; without them they may still display periodic violence, but such violence is not likely to become as dangerous as if nations have a military capacity. Using a national model — if each American governor had nuclear missiles, bombers, etc. the United States would be even more dangerous than it now is. Police forces are needed to quell violence, but the training and the weapons of police should be different from that of the military. Police should do all they can to *avoid* killing. Armies are trained *to* kill. Tranquilizing gas might be appropriate for some *police* action, but war systems with their mission of killing and destroying find it appropriate to invent any conceivable diabolic instrument biological, chemical, or nuclear, to maximize destructive capacity.

Applied to the international level, an international *police* force would be required for quelling violence between nations or for keeping violence to a minimum level until legal adjudication-mediation procedures were used. This would not be a world of absolute safety, but it probably would be a world where large scale violence was managed in a far safer way than it now is.

The economic advantages of moving from military systems to an international police system are enormous. Of the approximately 180 billion dollars per year now spent globally on all military systems, probably 160 billion could be diverted back into domestic needs. 20 billion per year is a rough estimate of the costs of an international peace-keeping system, including the political, legal, and economic machinery. Military expenditures under our old system have been continually rising throughout the world, cutting heavily into capital needed for economic development, and heavily into current consumer needs.

The escalation of terror that led us to this precarious period of history can be deescalated. But it can occur only if we can stand somewhat outside of the systems we have created so we can understand them. For example:

1. Country x wants to protect itself, so it develops a *defense* system.

2. Country y perceives of the action of country x as *offensive* and provocative. Therefore country y expands its defense system.

3. Country x perceives of the action of country y as offensive and provocative. Therefore country x expands its defense system.

4. Reciprocal escalation continues indefinitely until accident, miscalculation, madness or preventive war (for whatever motive) stops the process.

The previous scenario is probably at the core of the American-Russian and Russian-Chinese escalation of terror. Each side perceives of the other's actions as provocative and of its own as defensive. When the psychology of the system is understood it can be used to reverse the process.

1. Country x wants to protect itself, so it reduces some of its overkill capacity.

2. Country y perceives of the action as threat reducing. It sees no need to pay the economic price of a high threat level if country x sees no need, so it reduces its overkill at least equal to the level of country x.

3. Country x now feels encouraged by the threat reduction of country y and makes another arms reduction.

4. Country y reciprocates in kind, etc.

Charles Osgood has developed a detailed set of these psychological strategies that he calls "unilateral initiatives."[3] They are based on the psychological understanding of the processes operating on both sides, rather than on a nationalistic, two "player" psychology on which arms races are based. The conventional view that you cannot bargain except from a position of strength is sometimes workable, but it usually keeps mutual suspicion levels high and minimizes the possibilities of arms reduction. Americans can then be convinced that you can't trust the Russians, and the Russians can be convinced that you can't trust the Americans. Yet trust is a prerequisite to negotiation.

The unilateral initiatives that can encourage arms reduction are likely to be effective only to a limited degree. Unless an international or supranational system of conflict management and peace keeping is developed, nations must finally rely on the old pre-atomic national systems. Unilateral initiatives should therefore be part of a strategy for creating an atmosphere conducive to completing multi-lateral disarmament with phased simultaneous development of an international system of national defense. If the United States really wishes to have a defense system appropriate to the nuclear age, the SALT (Strategic Arms Limitations Talks) objectives should be seen to be entirely inadequate, merely a gesture toward stopping the arms race and retaining the status quo. Unilateral arms reduction initiatives and support of a revised United Nations charter similar to the Clark-Sohn plan would be a more substantive indication of American interest in an effective plan for survival.

THE NEED FOR A JOLT

Unless more Americans come to believe that their foreign policy and defense policy has been either very dangerous or morally wrong (or both) they are not likely to perceive of the *need* for reassessment. Any set of habits that seem to work are likely to persist, and the meaning of "it has worked" can be adapted to nearly any circumstances. The deterrence policy can be said to have worked because we have not had World War III. The Vietnam policy can be said to have worked because the communists have not taken over all of Vietnam.

Survivors of World War III are not likely to claim that the old system worked. But most Americans continue to have faith in the old ways, especially in the infinite powers of technology and the skills of management, with one possible exception— *Vietnam.*

There is a remote chance that Americans can learn enough from the Vietnam catastrophe to ask where they went off the track. To achieve this awareness it is crucial that Americans have *no* feeling of victory, honor, or success in Vietnam. For an American President to give the impression that the United States can extricate itself with "honor" is to nullify the single valuable potential of the Vietnam war — to force Americans into an awareness that this war has been a moral and political catastrophe born from the policies and habits of a potentially great nation that has become fundamentally irresponsible — a threat to itself and the human race. Such a rebirth of awareness and new commitment will require the trauma of defeat. America lacks the perspective of a country that has experienced victory but not defeat, for this has encouraged a pathological confidence and self-righteousness.

The massacre at My Lai, reported late in 1969, 20 months after it occured, shocked many Americans. The massacre was rationalized as an isolated incident, a reflection only on the individual soldiers who committed it, not on American policy — and it was dismissed with a view that "their massacres are worse than our massacres." But some Americans are likely to lose their self-righteous innocence and see that My Lai was only one of hundreds, possibly even thousands of similar incidents, committed by ground and air forces. The "My Lai" incident forces people to perceive of the brutal consequences of war, while bombing by high flying B 52's permits the same consequences but makes them psychologically remote, in which the killing of civilians can be called accidental. But the My Lai massacre has been unequivocally labeled *murder,* and there is hope that the rest of the war will also be perceived as *murder* and *large scale* massacre.

There have been many other war crimes committed by Americans in Vietnam, but the My Lai massacre is known throughout the world. After World War II the victorious allies were anxious to try the axis powers for war crimes and the United States encouraged the United Nations to affirm the principles of the Nuremberg Tribunal, which made *individuals* responsible for war crimes under international law. International law does not excuse crimes from one side on the basis that such crimes have also been committed by the other side; i.e. two wrongs do not make a right.

If the American government really believes in law and order it should

124

initiate a war crimes trial for American conduct in Vietnam. If the American government supports the blatant hypocrisy that punitive law should apply only to the other side it will be necessary for American citizens and other countries to initiate war crimes trials. Richard Falk, an international lawyer, has already outlined the basis for the application of the Nuremberg principles in Vietnam.[4] He has explained the responsibilities of both the combatants and the war planners and the need for them to punish war crimes or be themselves a party to the crime.

The brutal disregard for civilians is tied to such American policies as counterinsurgency warfare, and if investigations are made to document all alleged war crimes, the American people will be confronted by a specter of gross immorality similar to the Germans after World War II. Since the United States has a democratic structure, the personal responsibilities will be even greater.

World War III could consist of My Lai multiplied a *million* times. The psychological mechanisms of depersonalization and the technological remoteness of the consequences of most modern warfare have helped keep our obsolete defense systems intact. The pictures in *Life* magazine of the corpses of murdered My Lai women and children have made the present and future meaning of current American policy more vivid to many Americans.

There is no basis for confidence that the trauma necessary for fundamental reexamination of American foeign policy will necessarily emerge from the Vietnam war. The same policies underlying the cold war for the last 25 years still persist. While Chinese rhetoric is far more aggressive than Chinese action, American action is more aggressive than American rhetoric. The official American claims to peace, disarmament, and world law are contrasted by a continued policy of economic penetration, political subversion, and protracted conflict supported by conventional and nuclear military power. The most promising negotiations, the Strategic Arms Limitations Talks are aimed only at stabilization and minor reduction of the arms race with the Soviet Union. If this goal is achieved, the basic policies, values, and strategies of the Cold War could still continue, and the lesson of Vietnam may only be that interventionism should be more carefully planned hereafter.

The People's Republic of China's admission to the United Nations constitutes an important achievement for producing a representative U.N. But the United States deserves no credit for the achievement. The U.S. led the resistance to admission for over twenty years.

The needed changes will not come easily, but if Vietnam does produce a new capacity for critical reflection the following assessment of American foreign policy might be considered. These counter propositions are probably as supportable as any on which American foreign policy has been based since World War II. Their plausibility may increase in direct proportion to the need for reassessment of the cold war period.

1. Americans are partially, if not largely responsible for the cold war.

2. Communism offers a useful ideology for certain people whose history and circumstances have excluded western liberalism as a present viable choice.

3. Our own international behavior has betrayed our liberal creed and has become an agent of coercion, based largely on the metaphysics and the technology of militarism.

4. Because of the burgeoning immensity of American military power and because of the dominance of a military outlook, American self-righteousness has become one of the most dangerous forces in the world.

5. National defense based on national military power no longer provides national security but rather national insecurity.

6. Our deterrence policy and our peace through strength strategy has been a dangerous fantasy which threatens the existence of the human race.

7. The myth that our policy is only based on external realities ignores the ways in which American policy interprets the world through its own ideology and then helps create those realities.

A NEW AMERICA: RECONSTRUCTIVE PLANNING

Most Americans have been victims of their own culture. People in all countries are largely acting out the roles and supporting the values they have been conditoned to accept, but Americans, with their superior military and technological power, are playing the most dangerous game.

North America has been conquered (the Indians and the land) by a restless and often ruthless expansionism undergirded by Puritan values, applied science, and a market economy. Puritan values which our forebears were certain had cosmic sanction, have stressed the importance of work as a way of life and a superiority of man over nature. Knowledge has focused on an applied science that can exploit nature and produce individual wealth. The market economy has emphasized protestant individualism and survival-of-the-fittest competition. Each cultural system produces its own type of ''success'' and American success has been largely a function of these historical values.

There is enormous inertia in a culture. American institutions continue to be dominated by these old values, and they are likely to continue until it is realized that the old forms of success are no longer desirable nor even *possible.*

The American way has been the most effective instrument for the exploitation of nature and for the gross quantitative accumulation of wealth that the world has ever seen. The Gross National Product has been used as the primary indicator of national achievement. This consists of a quantitative scale that combines the total dollar units of goods and services. Its very composition reflects the lack of qualitative standards for it lumps together the total dollar units of cigarette commercials and cancer therapy; automobile sales and mortuary fees; napalm and sulfa drugs.

The Twentieth century has been labeled by Michael Harrington as "The Accidental Century", a century devoid of integrated social and economic planning. Faith in manifest destiny and inevitable progress has encouraged the belief that when American institutions get into trouble they will inevitably come out smelling like roses. Planning has been primarily individual planning or short range institutional planning.

But one form of planning has begun — a particular kind of planning that minimizes change in traditional values. John Galbraith in *The New Industrial State* described industrial planning that is aimed at anticipating market trends and then adapting to them or else at manipulating the public into the acceptance of products that may serve the corporation at the expense of the public.

Government planning has become similar, usually with less anticipation of trends and more reliance on ad hoc crisis treatment. But the goals have been based, as in industry, on what is technologically possible (the moon trip by NASA), whether or not it consisted of a sensible relative allocation of national resources. There is very little *social* planning in the United States, but what does exist in the larger institutions is either based on the manipulation of public consent or on the anticipation of trends. People are adjusted to institutions, seldom are institutions adjusted to people. *Yet the survival of mankind depends on planning which is based on ecology and which also gives people control over their future institutions and their values.* This requires moving from accidental change to the intentional control of change, and it requires a new education.

RECONSTRUCTIVE VS EXPANSIVE PLANNING

The only planning available to a society which has not developed qualitative social standards is *expansive* planning, by which an industry plans to sell *more* goods, schools plan to graduate *more* students, cities get *larger* and the buildings get *higher.* The linear quantitative direction of American society is supported by the "religion" of techno-fanaticism and "moneytheism."

Any form of planning increases predictability, and expansive planning increasingly permits us to tell young people that they should prepare for certain types of jobs because these will constitute the "manpower" needs of the near future. The enterprising citizen in such a system should prepare himself to be more marketable. Then he is a ''good'' citizen and he is likely to become ''successful.'' Our educational system, in both the classroom and the counselling office, reinforces this.

Expansive planning requires information about trends. It requires data to plot the rate and direction of change, but it assumes that people must adapt to the direction of change. It does not assume that the direction of change might be wrong and that the forces of social change should be more fundamentally controlled by people. Therefore, population expansion, technological development, and profit making create change to which *people* should adapt. Such planning aims neither at integrated planning nor in the reform of the forces of expansion.

Reconstructive planning carries us to a new societal stage. It requires a new education to initiate it and it reeducates those who become involved in it. It assumes that what is needed is not mainly planning *for* the future, but planning *of* the future. It assumes that trends should be adjusted to people rather than people to trends. It requires anticipation not only of trends but *illumination of the varieties of possible futures,* so that people can plan to have the kind of society they really want. It requires more integral social planning and a shift to macrocosmic science rather than microcosmic science. The inextricable connection between man and his environment requires the maximum use of ecology, which is the most integrative science. Knowledge that is organized into compartmentalized subject areas, as it usually is in schools, has little use in reconstructive planning.

Reconstructive planning moves beyond band-aid ad hoc treatment of social problems to consider the possible need for more fundamental reforms of social sub-systems. It aims at looking at the total system, not primarily for increasing technical efficiency — but for survival and for improving the quality of life.

Reconstructive planning will require information specialists but it will also require planners who can, in the context of a participatory process, take account of basic human values. Such a planner may need to combine the talents of a technician, an ecologist, and a humanist.

Our national defense system is part of the old world of expansive planning, which encourages burgeoning armament throughout the world. If present trends continue $4 *trillion* will be spent globally in the 1970's, depressing economic development everywhere.[5] The expanding national military systems will recruit and conscript millions of young men. The smaller nations will move toward overkill capacity while ''advanced'' nations escalate overkill.

Reconstructive planning would not expand the war making capacity of present systems but would move toward the development of a system of international conflict management based on world law. The goal would be to *avert,* cataclysmic war, therefore the means would not include merely increasing the technology of cataclysm by expanding present systems but rather by reconstructing present political and legal systems so that an effective international peace keeping system can operate.

EDUCATION AS SOCIAL EXPERIENCE

Neither a laissez faire society nor one based on expansive planning has a basis for identifying relevant *social* goals. In a laissez faire system the goals are individual. In an expansive system the goals are corporate, quantitative and technical — the power to achieve goals becomes a goal in itself.

Reconstructive planning assumes that the *processes* in which people become involved *constitute* their *education.* Education cannot be allocated to what are called schools while economic, military, and political institutions are treated as separate units of the society. People should not be mere instruments that add to the efficiency of the social ''machine.'' People become what they do, they are transformed by the roles and the experiences and the kind of society in which they live. This is the way cultures acquire their persistent conservatism — the young have been inducted from birth and they want to perpetrate the kind of meaning-structure which they have been taught is ''normal.''

If a culture is suicidal, as our pre-atomic culture now is, it requires extraordinary insight, new theory, and great initiative to make an intentional qualitative transformation of the culture. *But even to understand the old culture is to begin that transformation* — for the perpetration of a culture is based on its being *believed* — the transformation is based on its being *understood.*

To understand ones' culture it is useful to have experience in other ways of living, in other value systems. Cross-cultural and cross valuational experiences can result from living in other countries, with a different social class, and through art and literature that has explored other ways of living.

We need to understand where our society is going and to see what the alternatives are. This requires predictive information based on current trends. It requires the illumination of other possible future societies to make them as meaningful as possible. We must begin to design the future that makes the most sense and then engage in the educational and political action which will bring it into being.

MAN IN NATURE

The Judeo-Christian emphasis upon man's dominion over nature, has sanctioned the support of an arrogant and suicidal exploitation of nature. Whereas many other cultures begin with the assumption that man is part of nature and should seek a harmony with nature — western man's belief that he stands above nature has led him to rape and exploit it. What is now needed is a reconstruction of man's relation to nature. We need a revolution (already underway in Western Theology) departing from the man-nature dualism and using the new science of ecology. Lake Erie is virtually dead, forests are dying from smog, birds are dying of pollution, and yet man is part of the life chain. Man will either be forced into a new relationship with nature or will perish from his ignorance. Actually what is needed is a return to a very old relationship.6

The United States, the number one nation in gross national product, is also the number one nation in gross pollution and exploitation of nature. The current expansive planning takes little or no account of ecological responsibility. When Ford executives planned for the development and marketing of the Mustang they gave their consideration to corporate profits rather than to the questions of whether the internal combustion engine and the automobile (a major source of pollution) should continue to be the dominant form of transportation. Without reconstructive planning they helped guarantee the continued tyranny of the automobile. Without a new form of planning the old form will continue by default, blindly failing to recognize that by destroying nature man destroys himself.

THE QUEST FOR RELEVANCE

The word ''relevance'' is increasingly used by those who want to change the existing social order (which is increasingly becoming disorder). The use of the term ''relevance'' suggests that the present society is not sufficiently meaningful and that people have some sense of the direction change should take. In general, we might say that a society and the educational experiences it provides are ''relevant'' when they have a vital connection either to the conditions which sustain life or to the conditions which give life meaning. Modern America is increasingly a system that threatens more than it sustains life and that deprives people of meaning, since it substitutes a predatory paranoid culture for one that is life affirming and coherent. A leading organization in the peace movement has quite rightly asked for ''A Sane Nuclear Policy.''

A society that substitutes techno-fanaticism and profit making for environmental quality and social justice is one that persists in being irrelevant to many current human needs and one that provokes a sense of growing despair about the future. A society that is so locked into its old habits that it cannot even take human survival seriously is desperately irrelevant.

If the American people can begin to make headway toward reconstructive planning they may find that the central areas of concern might include (1) survival, (2) social justice, and (3) environmental quality. There is the danger that as we separate problems we may neglect their interrelatedness, yet programs for change must have focus toward problems. Planning directed toward *survival* would minimize the chances of unnecessary death; toward *social justice* it would minimize human exploitation; and toward *environmental quality* it would increase the desirability of living in a particular social-physical environment.

The current quest for relevance is itself an indication of the ever growing desire to order social priorities. Reconstructive planning requires that people attempt to agree on the kind of future they really wish, and this involves ordering priorities. Martin Luther King understood not only the need for social justice but he also saw that unless international violence could be controlled there would be little victory in the integration of radioactive corpses. If existence does precede essence — (physical life is a pre-requisite to social quality) — a perspective must be developed which will give relative emphasis to social goals and the allocation of time and energy to achieve them. In an age when pre-atomic war systems threaten the existence of the human race, anti-war planning should be given a top priority. But neither in a laissez faire system nor an expansive planning system is there a basis for this kind of historical-global comparative perspective. Expansive systems keep men locked into the old goals. The institution becomes king and the people become the pawns. Compare the relative effort the United States puts into the expansion and development of the present war system versus the effort put into disarmament negotiation and international peace keeping plans. R&D (Research and Development), now serving expansive planning almost exclusively, is equally needed for reconstructive planning.

BREAKING THE MOLD: SOME STRATEGIES

To break the constrictions of habits that have become pathological it is necessary to focus on the gulf between the kind of world we might have and the world that is. The possible world of the future should not be described, as it usually is, merely by the technologists. It must also be described by the artists, the conservationists, the people who are exploited within the present society. The rich, the poor, and the "silent majorities" must begin to dream of the kind of life they would really wish to have through an open dialogue of proposals, models, visions. The citizens then become artists rather than merely "manpower". Visions of the future need to be based on what is ecologically possible. As goals are clarified, focus can be given to social priorities.

Social assessments rather than Gross National Products should become the central indicators of national progress. Such assessments would need to compare the social consequences of 80 billion a year spent for instruments of war and annihilation versus the consequences if such funds were spent for hunger, sickness, and a "war" on ignorance.

The idea industries — schools, universities, R&D industries, and communication media — have a crucial role in shifting to a reconstructive society. Currently they contribute primarily to the expansive systems of the old order, but there is some indication that there is a growing awareness that the problems we are developing are problems of human survival. Even the affluent live increasingly in a world of crime, congestion, pollution, ugliness, and war. The disintegrating present is part of the misplanned past, and fundamental reform has advantages for everyone.

Criticism is the distinguishing feature of an intellectually open society, but the mass media have been as derelict as the schools in accepting the obligation for basic criticism. That is beginning to change — one of the few valuable bi-products of the Vietnam war. One salutatory effect of the Johnson administration in the area of foreign policy was to force schools and mass media more into the role of independent critics instead of faithful loyalists. When the theatre of the absurd gave regular performances on capital hill, the message was finally received.

What is now needed is to carry on the same spirit of criticism that has been directed primarily toward the Vietnam war and to extend it into all areas of American society. Without discriminating between the sense and the nonsense that constitutes the American heritage, people are swept by the flood of history and lack the basis for diverting the flow. As the processes of criticism become sufficiently basic, the mass media and the schools themselves can be subjected to criticism that can transform them into instruments of liberation instead of instruments of suppression. Then the cycle of ignorance, so essential to the maintenance of the old way of life, can be broken.

But new visions are not sufficient. People must increase their power to change institutions. The draft, military interventionism, and civil rights issues have helped politicize a society that previously slumbered in political apathy. Under the old order people had been *taught not* to be political. Those who used their constitutional rights had often been branded as un-American and had their jobs threatened and often eliminated.

To be political should not only be a right, but an obligation. Anything less implies that normal behavior does not involve participation in the control of change. In most of American society, industry and the military are prime examples, roles are allocated by an elite and participation in the change of the institution is tightly regulated (virtually forbidden in the military). Participation in change not only integrates a society, though not without conflict, but it breaks down the rigidified structures of institutions. It forces the institutions to serve people and constitutes a basic strategy for continuous change rather than the periodic revolutionary violence that becomes necessary when institutional rigidity persists too long.

The American military constitutes a totalitarian ghetto, and is one of the prime examples of non-reconstructionist education. Instead of participation, obedience is taught. Instead of criticising and choosing between value systems, ideological indoctrination is used. The soldier is identified as "manpower," a cog in the military machine. The kind of education provided by military experience is fundamentally in opposition to the kind of reconstructive education that is needed. That is why the first three chapters of this book focused on the military as the best example of a negative educational model — one that dehumanizes and is committed to expanding technology and expansive planning for war-making purposes. In searching for an education for survival it is useful to have a clear model of education for annihilation.

132

Military structures should be among the first priority targets for change toward a reconstructive society; the draft which supports such a system is a vital link in keeping the military system intact. The funds that congress appropriate are equally necessary. The abrogation of a citizen's constitutional rights within present military systems; these are all ways in which present military systems are perpetuated. Appropriate political action requires the reversal of the support systems and the creation of viable plans for a system of conflict management appropriate to the atomic age.

The record of public irresponsibility is so great on the part of many profit making businesses that it encourages people to recommend economic systems that allow for no profit making at all. But there are some profit making areas that are not predatory, and a participatory and reconstructive society would have to work out experimentally a new balance between private profit and public interest. What is clear in American society is that business activities must be far more circumscribed by public control. The use of natural resources cannot be determined primarily by profit in the market place. Many resources are scarce and irreplacable. Commerce must not determine where it is necessary to live — it must move to where people desire to live. People have been forced to live where jobs are available. This is currently a major problem of the burgeoning metropolis. Entire cities need to be planned anew, taking account of the ecology and the human conditions for a good society. The economic considerations of a scarcity economy has determined where our cities are now located. Business must therefore follow, not determine, social objectives that take account of the esthetic, religious, social, economic, and ecological needs that should henceforth underly the plans for the future. The transformation of the present economic system will be no easy matter, for the ideology supportive of the old order is taught by and transmitted through the immense power of profit-making business. When business men say that they are only giving people what they want, they themselves often fail to admit that the system has taught them what to want.

To unlock present businesses from the military-industrial complex will be no easy matter. Profit making and war-making have become fused into a way of life. Jules Henry, an anthropologist, points out:

"Anthropologists studying the rise of religions discovered long ago that people come to adore whatever gives them livelihood ... We invest by far the greatest part of our national treasure in the means of creating devastation and death, which in turn gives most of us, at whatever cost, unprecedented prosperity — so the means for mass death becomes sanctified and patriotic."[7]

Replanning must therefore be realistic about the ideological obstacles that must be overcome. One is the myth that a war system produces prosperity. It temporarily stimulates the economy and provides immense profits to a few, but it fails to provide the more useful long run forms of investment capital and it wastes the resources and energies of a nation in anti-social activity. The result is a *decline* in the rate of growth even of the quantitative gross national product, plus inflated prices for consumer's goods.

One irony of American life is that the official ideology describes a largely free-enterprise economy, while in fact both business and government have created a form of socialism for the rich through the military industrial complex.[8] Businesses seem quite ready to sacrifice the old ideology when it is profitable to do so, but public policy has made it more profitable to support war systems than peace systems. If labor and industry are to disconnect themselves from a war system there will have to be equally attractive plans for gaining livelihood in other ways. This means that peace plans must be at least as well developed and reliable as the war plans on which the American economy has been so largely based. Labor and industry are not likely to be a political hindrance to reconstructive planning if it can be as economically rewarding as the old system, and there is no reason why it cannot be. In fact, the Net National Product (social gains minus social loss) would increase considerably. But a war based economy cannot be dismantled without simultaneous substitution of a peace economy. This requires as much attention to peace planning as the Pentagon provides for war planning.

TEACHING PLANNING THROUGH THE SCHOOLS

Schools have reinforced the old order mainly by failing to illuminate alternatives. They have also been directly a part of the war system, working on war research and training military officers in ROTC programs. They have also contributed to the old order by reinforcing expansive systems and preparing technically trained manpower for the job market. The label "liberal arts" has usually been given to irrelevant, trivial, upper class leisure-status activities.

Elementary schools and high schools have been largely dominated by the colleges and the universities. The teachers are products of higher education and most of the materials they use are developed by professors in ideological cooperation with publishing industries. Higher education usually has cast the shadow of darkness on the lower school.

Possibly the most basic problem is the lack of relevance of schools to the dominant issues of our age. Students, rather than faculty, have led the revolt against irrelevance, but an increasing minority of faculty are also trying to focus on the kind of knowledge that permits intelligent participation in social change.

When knowledge is organized in such a manner as to hinder people from having control over the power structure that supports their social order, the result is to reinforce the status quo. The phrase "knowledge explosion" usually refers to the kind of knowledge that serves expansive planning. Most of this knowledge is atomistic, technical, and usable within existing institutional structures. Teaching machines and the "new" math, science, and social science have focused primarily on academic knowledge with minimum relevance to the central human problems of our age. Virtually none of the exploding knowledge treats alternative strategies for war prevention. Much of it provides the mathematical and scientific know how to expand the efficiency of current war systems.

Education for survival clearly requires a reversal of these trends. Reconstructive planning needs to be at the center rather than the periphery of the curriculum. Knowledge should be mainly organic, integrative, and ecological. The focus should be on identifying the central problems of the future as they are developing in the present and on gaining the knowledge that permits people to control institutions and technology.

The old order has been based not only on what we have done but also on how we have done it. The way in which we have come to think and live has been reinforced by the schools. We put life into compartments, for specialization has increased industrial efficiency. We have disintegrated the human personality and made it impossible for such schools to integrate the society. Knowledge is compartmentalized (by subjects), thought and emotion is separated (learn now, do later). Experience is cut up into time slots (courses) so that real problems must be avoided, since it is not possible to specify the exact time for social projects to come to fruition.

Education for reconstructive planning requires integration of thought and emotion, theory and practice, and it requires continuity of experience. It does not preclude specialization, but it does preclude merely specializing. We should no longer develop a trained cripple to fit into a dehumanized society, but we continue to do it in virtually all schools, particularly in the Armed Forces. The person who is to participate in the development of a humane society must be helped to become a whole person in relation to nature, society, and himself.

Fortunately young people are increasingly able to develop their own culture and escape from the miseducation of the old order. It is important that such youth gain positions of power in educational institutions to replace the ''neutral'' technician of the older generation who has shown himself to be politically bankrupt.

NEUTRALITY AND OBJECTIVITY

One of the major myths of universities is the belief in the value of ''objectivity,'' by which the scholar is presumed to be morally neutral and concerned only with truth. This view is itself part of the ideology of the old order, for it excuses the scholar and researcher from having a theory of social relevance and it permits him to be accountable only to scientific standards of research methodology and the judgment of his peers, who are usually success products of the same system.

The knowledge used in reconstructive planning should be scientific and accurate, and the highest standards of intellectual honesty and the best methods of obtaining accurate information must be used. The new focus of inquiry, however must be shifted to a different set of questions and knowledge must be aimed at functional integration rather than atomism, at problems of collective survival and social justice rather than merely academic problems. The intellectual process either reinforces the social order or opens up alternative solutions — its structure is part of the social order, and it can reconstruct that order only by reconstructing itself.

For example: From 1968 to 1970 at the University of Hawaii a small group of students and faculty began to focus on futurism and planning. Central attention was given to the kind of Hawaii that was possible by the year 2000 and the kind of Hawaii that was developing. What had been developing was air, water, and noise pollution. Obsolete transportation systems and uncontrolled expansion had reduced the esthetic and social quality of life. It had glutted the roads with traffic and created some of the world's highest housing costs. All these problems were illuminated by these faculty planners and students, and the local papers not only gave coverage to planning proposals but they were highly supportive of the new interests in futurism.

The pressures had political repercussions and more attention was given by the Governor and the legislature to planning questions. By early 1970 there was evidence that planning would be the central political issue of the next election, and though the problems of reconstructive planning were only beginning to be considered, the university was starting to shift toward planning considerations and many of the problems were seen to be unsolvable without more integral reconstructive planning. At least a small part of the university was therefore beginning to effect virtually all institutions in the state, not by being ''neutral'' but by being responsible and relevant. The old neutrality had been one of the reasons for the problems.

When the planning frame of reference expands beyond the local area, as it must, then the problems of war, population, pollution of the planetary biosphere, and sharing of the resources of the earth become interrelated problems. The needed political and legal reform become planning problems — therefore they become educational problems. Soon the university contributes to man's progress and survival in the nuclear era and it begins to cast light instead of a shadow on pre-college education and the surrounding community.

CULTURAL RECONSTRUCTION

Reconstructive planning involves cultural reconstruction. It involves change in the power structure, social structure, and ideology of a nation. Most American schools are themselves so much a part of the culture that they selectively omit the kind of study that provides a critical awareness of the way in which the society is ordered, the way in which values are usually shaped, and the specific values that constitute the American way of life. So Americans tend to universalize the beliefs that they have been taught, since they have no way of distinguishing between human nature and the particular values of their own culture.

They often proclaim that man is *naturally* aggressive, *naturally* competitive, and *naturally* self-interest motivated. To these assumptions about human nature are added other myths about natural rights of individuals and "laws" of supply and demand which are presumed to be part of nature.

These notions, are often treated as absolutes, as metaphysical laws and therefore they are held with self-righteous certainty. Such piety not only inhibits the reconstruction of the culture but it encourages a self-righteous foreign policy that becomes more concerned with the techniques of implementation than with the justification of the goals.

Other ways of life are perceived as inferior. Other political and economic forms are perceived as wrong, and foreign policy becomes a holy war. Students from our "leading" universities have generally found it easy to serve government or industry and to fit into the life style and the mythology, because the schools have seldom served the very process of criticism that might make them contributors to an open democratic society. They usually serve the objective of understanding democratic political *forms* without creating cultural awareness and without opening up a radical range of value alternatives. The student is supposed to feel "free" (to get a job) when he has the diploma and certification, though he is still locked into the ubiquitous value system of the culture.

It would be an exaggeration to claim that virtually no student escapes. Increasingly they do escape, often forming various kinds of counter cultures — radical reformist — alienated escapist — as the case may be. But the counter cultures too often consist of absolutistic negations of conventional values. The real educational revolution would be for schools to maximize student awareness of current cultural values and help students design preferred futures, and create change through social action.

Visions for new futures require new experience. The study and even the direct experience of non-western cultures would be useful to westerners. But direct experience and study of the various ethnic varieties within the western world itself can be helpful. The differences between lower and middle class life styles in the local "community" (as we erroneously call it) should be a normal part of American education.

The role of ideology is conspicuously neglected in most schools. Economics is often taught as a value-neutral science, even though the actual use of economics must always be within a cultural-political-ideological context. Students of economics are usually naive about the goals their technical knowledge will be serving, and so we typically prepare technicians rather than participants in cultural reconstruction. The study of comparative ideology opens up new alternatives.

Most American schools substitute the state for the church, especially in elementary schools, and carry on a certain amount of direct indoctrination of nationalism. In high school, and even more so in colleges

137

and universities, the indoctrination is less direct. It occurs primarily through omission of criticism of established institutions and the omission of a world perspective. The content of *academic subjects* is studied rather than the cultural content of one's society.

The war-system has a pervasive effect on all of American life, and yet the nationalistic assumptions, the human-nature myths, and the economic-educational complex that supports it and that pervades its ideology are in a virtually total state of neglect throughout most American education. If half as much time were spent studying the assumptions on which American militarism is based as is spent on indoctrinating young men into military systems through Jr. and Sr. ROTC, the curriculum of American schools would be substantially modified.

The great disparity in the distribution of wealth within the United States and between countries is supported by very questionable, but seldom questioned, ideologies. The schools should help students examine the ways in which ideology and culture are related to power and privilege. Even those who are exploited usually accept the ideologies which support their exploitation. Until Americans have a basis for questioning the assumptions upon which their own mal-distribution of wealth are based they are hardly in a position to serve as anything except an obstacle in reconstructing economic systems throughout the world.

PARTICIPATING IN CHANGE

The old order is supported by the atomistic organization of knowledge (separate subjects), by illusions of objectivity, and by avoidance of a critical study of society, but it is also supported by a separation of knowledge and practice. The old order allocates thinker-technicians to some roles and allocates workers to others. Reconstructive planning requires direct knowledge of alternative systems and experience participating in change.

Ralph Nader's "raiders" provide an excellent model of participative education. Law students voluntarily join him in investigating ways in which industry and government exploit the public. When he has the evidence to expose a department of government or industry, he becomes directly involved in political action by effectively lobbying and use of mass media. None of this is outside the legitimate functions of educational institutions. Students should be encouraged to give careful attention to what they think is really in the public interest. But unless they are investigating real institutions and trying to change them they are isolated from the active side of social change that is essential to their education.

At earlier ages students can investigate problems such as water and air pollution and then inquire into the reasons for the problem. They may discover that there is a lack of appropriate legislation or that there is a lack of monitoring and enforcement, and they can illuminate the problem to the community. They will at least gain more understanding of pollution control and possibly help effect actual change.

Participation should not only be outside the school, but also within the school in all aspects of its governance. The old order is based on conditioning people to accept the traditional values and the elitist power systems of institutions. Reconstructive planning requires that institutions serve people and so schools that try to reconstruct society must also be willing to reconstruct themselves, encouraging students to share in the transformation of the schools.

The movement toward increased student participation in the governance of schools is well underway. The next priority is for faculty and students to transform the subject matter so that it contributed to the transformation of the larger society.

If schools emphasized reconstructive education as it has been proposed, they would do the following:

1. Focus on the future

2. Identify present trends

3. Reexamine cultural and existential goals

4. Learn the ecological limits of choice

5. Emphasize world community

6. Build alternative models of the future

7. Identify preferred futures

8. Establish social change priorities

9. Participate in the implementation of plans

10. Reassess on the basis of subsequent experience

Schools in America have supported the old cultural values of individualism by perpetuating self-interest, in the reward structure and in the subject matter. The alternative is to identify public interest, which in our age is *world interest*. The failure of schools to pre-commit themselves to humanistic goals has hindered political consensus. It is as necessary to *precommit* education to aid in the elimination of war, ecocide, and poverty as it is for a medical school to commit itself to prolong human life rather than erradicating it.

With consensus on general survival and social justice goals we can concentrate on the *means* for achieving them, by which there can be honest and thoughtful disagreement. Such disagreement on means can be experimentally tested, however. There may be various ways to eliminate environmental destruction and poverty. The evidence can be evaluated to direct us toward more reliable common goals. The ideology of most current education is that it is ''open'' about both means and ends. When it is open about basic values of survival and human justice it is really indifferent to life, reinforcing the existing order in which economic values are primary. The prevailing ideology claims that schools should be intellectual not moral. Such an ideology is even common in university programs in the "humanities."

The following project is an example of humanistic pre-commitment. It is a project in a class titled "Education for a World Without War" in teacher education, taught by the writer. The class found that no political party or presidential candidate in the 1972 election had identified world interest goals. All had wanted to get out of the war in Vietnam, but none had advocated getting out of the *war-system.* So a statement was designed as a guideline for political change. It was sent to candidates, delegates, and political parties. But it was also treated as *curriculum material for use in the schools.* The objective was to be educational, action oriented, and yet to use systems change as the way to create world community and survival. The general *goals,* elimination of war, ecocide, and poverty, are treated as moral premises for all civilized people. Disagreement may well occur on *means,* which includes the specific items on the platform. But those who disagree on these specific items are morally obligated to offer better means. To be "neutral" is to reinforce present systems.

The project is offered as one specific example of how to practice education for survival. (The project may be used without permission, providing credit is given. Students involved in the project are listed in the source appendix.)9

A PROPOSAL FOR NEW POLITICAL GOALS TOWARD A FUTURE WITHOUT WAR

William Boyer, University of Hawaii

I

PREFACE TO PLATFORM

We believe that political candidates and parties must broaden their perspective and extend their goals to effect more fundamental change in the world system. Otherwise, the old system is perpetuated by default, retaining massive human injustice and insuring global catastrophe.

The present world system has three intolerable features.

1. It perpetuates the nation-state war system, even though atomic technology has made war obsolete by permitting mutual annihilation without defense.

2. It perpetuates a world system that permits individuals, corporations, and nations to make unilateral use of common, scarce, irreplaceable natural resources, resulting in destruction of the common environment on which all life depends.

3. It widens the gap between the rich and the poor throughout the world, hindering the development of human community, destroying human life, crippling human potentiality, and raising the probabilities that violence will be the dominant instrument of world wide social change.

Responsible politics must provide courses of action which will direct change toward the prevention of war, ecocide, and poverty; toward the creation of world community. This means that extrication from Vietnam is necessary but not sufficient, for the more basic problem is to plan in such a way as to transform the system on which war itself depends.

Political goals are inadequate if they fail to recognize the interrelationship between the future of nations and the future of all people. Unless national political parties advocate an integrated plan for global reform they lack the vision to speak relevantly to the crisis problems of our age.

There may be various means of achieving the larger goals of war prevention, resource management, and economic justice. The most plausible method is to extend law, order, and justice by creating representative global agencies. The United Nations structure could serve these objectives if the legislative, executive, and judicial roles were strengthened. Essentially it requires strengthening world law to provide the basis for crisis management and first steps toward world community instead of the current global anarchy.

There can be no effective world law without an effective World Court, and the present World Court is ineffective for various reasons, one being the Connally Amendment, which was introduced by the United States during the formation of the United Nations. It is clear that repeal of the Connally Amendment is necessary and should be included in the platform of all political parties.

Our proposals address themselves to foreign policy, but they are inextricably connected to domestic policy. The social and environmental needs of American society cannot be met until the war system is transformed into a peace-keeping system, with the savings transferred to serve the real needs of mankind.

The current administration's proposals to continue or expand high levels of military spending are a commitment to the status quo by keeping the present inadequate system intact. The United States should not unilaterally disarm without helping create a substitute system for conflict management and international peace keeping. But it is necessary to take *unilateral initiatives* to begin a reduction in the oversized American system. The American military system would continue to have *overkill* capacity even at a reduced level of support. Foreign policy initiates self-fulfilling prophecies — the United States can lead an arms race or lead in arms reduction. The goal is *multilateral* disarmament but responsible leadership has everything to gain and nothing to lose by taking moderate unilateral initiatives. The new relations with China have come from tension reduction overtures, not from threat.

The following platform proposals aim at the strengthening of world law and world community. This involves a shift from the use of a global threat system into a global peace-keeping system, assigning the transference of economic credits to social and environmental needs at both the domestic and international level. The separate platform items therefore have a systematic relationship.

II
THE NEED FOR NEW PLATFORM GOALS

Unless a national party or a national candidate speaks to the three problems of war, ecology, and poverty and treats them as world problems, we believe the statements of goals will be inadequate. Specifically, this means coming to grips with the following questions:

1. How can conventional national military systems be transformed into an international peace-keeping system?

2. How can the world biosphere be managed to prevent destruction of a common world environment?

3. How can an equitable world system of economic development be achieved which will rapidly eliminate poverty?

The achievement of these goals is possible with present levels of knowledge. What is needed is political action. We believe every national candidate is obligated to respond to these central issues, on which the future of man depends.

To indicate that dedication to the elimination of war, ecocide, and poverty can be supported by political action, we offer the following proposals which are specific enough to provide a basis for undertaking political action. If these proposals are rejected, it is however incumbent on a responsible candidate or party that other means be offered and defended which will be instrumental to the same goals of elimination of war, poverty, and ecocide.

SPECIFIC PROPOSALS

1. Support United Nations charter revision to provide for a standing police force, executive power to take action during threats to international peace, and World Court jurisdiction over settlement of international conflict.

2. Support repeal of the Connally Amendment, introduced in 1946 by the American Senate, which continues to cripple the World Court because it gives the United States the power to decide whether a dispute shall fall within the jurisdiction of the World Court. Other nations have used the Connally Amendment for their national objectives, restricting the legitimate jurisdiction of the World Court and contributing to its ineffectiveness.

3. Support world-wide multilateral disarmament and take unilateral initiative by reducing the size and the capacity of the American armed forces, which will merely reduce the present ''overkill'' capacity. Support an effective UN peace-keeping system so that *all* nations can *increase* their actual security while also being substantially relieved from the burden of an increasingly expansive nation-state military system, which is no longer capable of defending. Phase in the UN system as the national system is phased out.

4. Support a plan to convert the enormous world savings from disarmament into (a) multilateral development systems such as the UN Development Program, directed toward the elimination of world poverty, (b) domestic programs to support social and environmental needs. At least $70 billion would be available for both purposes since the war system costs the United States about 8% of the GNP while a UN peace-keeping system would require a contribution of no more than 1% of the American GNP.

5. Support a UN world environment commission to study and propose environmental legislation to be adopted by the general assembly and applied to international law through the World

Court. Laws for management, use, and control of the oceans could be a first objective.

6. Support change in American government (such as the creation of a Department of Peace) to provide transition management during the conversion to a peace system. Such a department should plan the economic conversion in the United States so that employment and prosperity is *increased* during the transference of military spending to peace spending. The Department of Peace should also sponsor education and research bearing on the new world goals and the problems of transition.

III
PLATFORM DOCUMENTATION

THE CONNALLY AMENDMENT

Because the potentially effective use of the International Court of Justice plays a primary role in the development of World Peace, the Connally Amendment, which limits the effectiveness of the Court, must be repealed.

The United States Declaration accepting the compulsory jurisdiction of the World Court in 1946 included the Connally Amendment which states:

"Disputes with regard to matters which are essentially within the domestic jurisdiction of the United States of America AS DETERMINED BY THE UNITED STATES OF AMERICA."

The implications of this "self-judging" clause are:

The United States can prevent adjudication in any case brought against it by claiming that the matter is within its domestic jurisdiction.

The United States is at a disadvantage in the World Court because by the principle of reciprocity any country can invoke the Connally Amendment against the United States. The Connally Amendment has been invoked either directly or reciprocally in every case where it was available — three cases to date.

Out of seven countries which copied the Connally Amendment, the United States is the only major power in the world to retain the "self-judging" clause, which negatively affects stature of the World Court.

According to the Charter of the International Court of Justice, Article 2 (7), the World Court is not able to intervene in essentially domestic American matters, so the Connally Amendment is not necessary.

There is a question as to the legality of the Connally Amendment:

Article 36 (6) of the Statute of the Court says: "In the event of a dispute as to whether the Court has jurisdiction, the matter shall be settled by the decision of the Court." Therefore, the Connally Amendment is invalid under International Law.

As early as 1946, and again in 1960, the American Bar Association favored the repeal of the Connally Amendment. Seven Judges on the World Court independently pronounced the Connally Amendment invalid.

It has not yet, however, been repealed by the United States Senate.

WORLD DEVELOPMENT AND MILITARY COSTS

The world is beset with economic problems. Even in the United States, there are many people who are isolated spatially, socially, and economically from the majority of Americans who live comfortable lives. The absolute poor are a minority in the United States but are the majority in the underdeveloped countries and in the world.

For decades there has been much talk about solving the world's poverty problems, but there has not been enough capital used for development purposes and too little effective action. Ten years ago, the United Nations declared the 1960's the Decade of Development, but this period was not successful because no comprehensive and far-reaching programs had been planned or initiated. Furthermore, the Western countries had become increasingly less inclined to provide foreign aid. The second Development Decade has been declared for the 70's but its success seems improbable if the political and social structures affecting it do not change.

Gunnar Myrdal, in *Challenge of World Poverty*, believes that the failure of world economic programs stem from the fact that they are piecemeal and blind to certain realities about the underdeveloped nations, which act as impediments to and even prevention of any pervasive change to improve the lot of the world's poor. He stresses the following three major problem areas which need to be recognized and solved before any type of successful world development is accomplished:

1. *There has not been any effective multilateral and equitable system of channeling and distributing the aid that is given to the UDC from another country.* International agencies have not had enough power to collect and distribute aid and resources equitably. Ninety percent of all aid is given unilaterally by the national government in the developed countries. Aid from developed nations is important but the form and distribution of that aid is crucial. In the past, much aid had been in the form of military armaments and/or monetary bribery for the UDC's political loyalty to the donor. The

145

U.S. aid to Laos, South Korea, and South Vietnam is an example of this type of military/political aid.

2. As important as foreign aid are the needed social and economic reforms within the underdeveloped countries themselves. Although the policy declarations of all underdeveloped countries favor greater equality, in practice, the economic and social inequality seems to be rising. This paradox is explained by the distribution of power in underdeveloped countries. "Political power in almost all underdeveloped countries is held by upper-class groups who have generally prevented effective reforms aimed at protecting and advancing the interests of the masses." The Western countries have neglected to promote necessary social reforms and have even discouraged them. Egalitarian reforms have proven to be beneficial to the developed Western countries, therefore, there should be more active support for the same kind of reforms to develop in the UDCs. Furthermore, at this time there is no central agency to administer foreign aid and resources in such a way that the masses of the UDC are ensured of direct benefits.

3. There is no central agency which can regulate transactions between developed countries' private businesses and the UDC's government. Direct business investment from developed countries has seldom been designed for creating greater equality. At most, Western business has pampered the already rich and added to the already complex problem of corruption in the government of these countries. "...in private conversations, they (businessmen) frankly admit that it is often necessary to bribe both high and low officials in order to run their enterprises without too many obstacles." (An example of just how far a business will go in tampering with the politics of another country, just to protect its business investments, is the allegation by Jack Anderson that secret papers from the ITT files reveal the political maneuverings ITT resorted to in an effort to stop the 1970 election of the leftist Chilean President Salvador Allende.)

The burden of military spending in poor countries and the use of human resources for war systems has caused the have-not countries to deplete their savings, which could have been invested in the countries' development and upgrading of living standards.

In the year 1967 (the latest year for which comprehensive data are available) the military expenditures of the world's nations totaled $182 billion. The example of military spending set by the developed countries is readily followed by the UDCs. The average expenditures per person in the UDC were about $5 per year for public education and $2 for public health. In 1966 the UDCs as a group *spent more on their military budgets than on government-supported education and public health combined:* $17 billion for the armed forces, therefore emphasis on military spending has absorbed the economic development of the poor nations.

THE DEVELOPMENT OF A DEPARTMENT OF PEACE

SPONSORING THE MOVE FOR PEACE

The United States is a world power that cannot shrug off nor delegate responsibility for world peace. America should set an example and initiate required actions that will convince the world that peace is possible. We cannot afford to sit back and believe that another nation will pick up the standard of "World Peace" and lead the way. Hawaii, for instance, the youngest State, now has the opportunity to move ahead and establish foundations for peace so urgently needed in this complex world. It is befitting that Hawaii, which suffered and endured the baptismal fire of World War II should lead a peace initiative. Let us begin by recognizing that an organization is urgently needed whose major concern lies in developing, promoting and establishing peace both in the United States and at the world level.

THE BILLS PRESENTED TO CONGRESS

Since two formal legislative bills have previously been introduced in Congress dealing specifically with the advancement of world peace, the most expedient means available of enhancing world peace is to support the existing bills. These bills are HR 12600 — introduced by Congressman Seymour Halpern and HR 208 — introduced by Congressman Spark Matsunaga.

The main proposal of the two bills cited is the development of a "Peace Department" at the national level. These proposals offer two separate courses of action, either a government organized Cabinet post called the "Department of Peace," or an independent organization for the development of peace. Without the benefit of experience, it is difficult to decide which course of action would be better. Yet the government organized cabinet appears to be the more feasible course of action. A new government Cabinet has the advantages in obtaining funds, manpower and material resources. The identical organizational structures proposed by both bills warrant serious attention. Selection of personnel to staff the various leadership positions proposed must be closely scrutinized for the power of the department depends largely on individuals who are interested and knowledgeable in providing the leadership vital to the achievement of world peace.

PROBLEM AREAS

As the HR 12600 Bill presented by Mr. Halpern to the 92nd Congress, 2d Session, represents basically the same proposals made by Mr. Matsunaga in his HR 208 presented to the same Congress, 1st Session, we will refer to both bills when we use the term "bill". The one exception to this referral will be in reference to Title III of the individual bills in question. Mr. Matsunaga's bill proposes a "Peace By Investment Corporation"; Mr. Halpern's bill proposes a "Joint Committee on Peace and International Cooperation." These two subjects differ greatly and should be dealt with separately. Our objective is to discuss only the concept of a "Department of Peace."

The bill will transfer to the Peace Department the functions of a number of existing agencies. Some argue that the existing agencies are adequate, yet little progress has been made. As the current system has not achieved any obvious success, it appears to be time to change this system. This change is not made merely for the sake of change, but rather in the belief that a Peace Department concept offers a new and more promising approach to world peace. If a Department of Peace could be as influential as the Department of Defense has been in guiding foreign policy and the State Department, we would experience a new era in world politics and a new opportunity to meet domestic needs.

WORLD ENVIRONMENT

Pollution of air and water is not merely an American problem nor is it a problem confined to nations. We live in a common biosphere that has no respect for national boundaries. The Rhine River flows past the potash mines of Alsace, through the industrial Ruhr Valley to the North Sea. Known as Europe's Sewer, the river is so toxic that even eels have difficulty surviving. The North American Great Lakes are victims of similar ecological irresponsibility, and the last of the lakes, Lake Erie, has become a putrified threat to the health of both Canada and the United States whose adjacent cities draw drinking water from a source that supports only the organisms compatible with sewage and industrial chemicals.

Sweden receives soot from England, and the United States and India have corrupted the entire world's oceans with DDT. Yet, man is utterly dependent on the common world ecosystem, which includes oceans, coastal estuaries, forests, topsoil, and grasslands. The web of interacting organisms form the rhythmic cycles and food chains within which life becomes possible.

Pollutants usually end in the oceans, which cover 70% of the globe. Yet, the oceans are limited to the amount and kind of pollutants they can absorb. Ecologists are concerned about effects on phytoplankton for 70% of the Earth's oxygen is produced by ocean phytoplankton, which supports animal life and the energy uses underlying industrial societies.

Though the world's biosphere is a system, the nations that exploit the biosphere are not yet part of a system. Unilateral exploitation is therefore inevitable without a common political system for planning the common use of the environment. The 1972 United Nations Conference on the Human Environment is a first step toward common ecological planning, but it requires national political support to become an effective instrument for world survival.

World Law supporting the environmental prerequisites to life is the central political need. Related research, education, and enforcement mechanisms are also necessary along with means to help make the economic transition from economies of exploitation and waste to economies that are constrained by ecological principles and are based on recycling of resources.

American politics has already started to become responsive to environmental needs by support of environmental education, environmental quality standards, and family planning. Such effort, however, is so minor compared to the problems that for each step that has been gained, two have been lost in the meantime. Environmentalists call the 1970's ''The Decade of Grace.'' This is our last chance to initiate national and global change appropriate to the problems or to load the dice for irreversible catastrophe.

Clearly we need:

1. Strong national and world environmental law.
2. An effective system of national and world enforcement.
3. Both national and world research and education on environmental planning.
4. Global planning for transition to an ecologically managed world economy, using law, economic rewards and punishments, and education to effect the transition.

BIBLIOGRAPHY

INTRODUCTION

1. Fulbright, J. William, *The Arrogance of Power,* Random House, New York, 1966.

CHAPTER I

1. See Barnet, Richard J., *The Economy of Death,* Atheneum, New York, 1969, pp. 57-128.
2. Elkin, Frederick, "The Soldier's Language," *American Journal of Sociology,* LI, 1946, p. 422.
3. Elkin, Henry, "Aggressive and Erotic Tendencies in Army Life," *American Journal of Sociology,* LI, 1946, p. 413.
4. ⸺, p. 410. ˙
5. 15-136 RPC Publishers Printing, Rogers Kellogg Corporation — L8-763-300M.
6. See *Military Leadership,* FM 22-100, 1961. Also, S. L. A. Marshall, *Men Against Fire,* Wm. Morrow, New York, 1947, p. 50.
7. ⸺, p. 64.
8. Leonard, Frank, *City Psychiatric;* reviewed by Saul Landau in *Ramparts,* Sept. 1965, p. 62.
9. *Honolulu Advertiser,* UPI Report, Oct. 1, 1965.
10. *The Progressive,* AP Report, Sept. 1965, p. 25.
11. See Isaac Deutscher, "October Revolution, New Style," *The Reporter,* Sept. 15, 1956, pp. 14-17.
12. See *Time,* Nov. 26, 1956, p. 24; also, Erich Fromm, *May Man Prevail,* 1961, p. 132.
13. See Chapter II.
14. Some of the founding fathers such as Thomas Jefferson made no connection between man's natural world and a supernatural source of authority for some were deists rather than monotheists.
15. Dept. of Defense, Office of the Armed Forces Information and Education, 1959, p. 103.
16. ⸺, p. 139.
17. See Fred Cook, *The Warfare State,* Macmillan, New York, 1962, pp. 278-283.
18. In a personal letter from General Krulak, Oct. 19, 1965. He has also made similar statements to the press.
19. General Krulak spoke as though he were an avowed anti-Communist - but committed the usual error of failing to understand that his type of military influence undermines some of the distinguishing features of American democracy and moves us closer to the very totalitarianism which is usually claimed to be the reason why we should fear Communism.
20. Published at public expense by the Superintendent of Documents, Washington, D. C.

21. Typically, the chapel is located on a military base, built and supported at public expense.
22. It is also compulsory for recruits of the three services to attend a "Character Guidance Program" prepared by a board of chaplains. It consists of indoctrination in "Godly patriotism."
23. *Builders of Faith,* Dept. of Defense, 0-749-616, 1965, p. 11.
24. ——————, op. cit., pp. 14-15.
25. *Chaplains of the United States Army,* Roy J. Honeywell, Col. Ret., Dept. of the Army, p. 339.
26. *Builders of Faith,* op. cit., p. 6.
27. Burchard, Waldo, "Role Conflicts of Military Chaplains," in J. Milton Yinger's *Religion, Society, and the Individual,* New York, 1957, p. 586.
28. Berger, Peter, *The Noise of Solemn Assemblies,* New York, 1961, p. 67.
29. Huie, William Bradford, *The Execution of Private Slovik,* New York, 1954, pp. 132-134.
30. Burchard, Waldo, *op.cit.* One conclusion of this study was that "for the chaplain, the role of military officer provides his primary identification," p. 589.
31. *In* Matthew, 19:18; Mark, 10:19; Luke, 18:20; Exodus, 20:13.
32. See Congressional Record-Senate, Feb. 18, 1969, SI 722-724.
33. Cook, Fred, *op. cit.,* Chapter IV.
34. ——————, p. 104.
35. Neblett, William H., *Pentagon Politics,* Pageant Press, New York, 1953.
36. "Armed Forces Information Program," *For Commanders,* Dept. of Defense, IV, Oct. 15, 1964, p. 4.
37. Hersh, Seymour, "The Great A.B.M. Pork Barrel," *War/Peace Report,* Jan. 1968, p. 4.
38. Cook, Fred, *op. cit.,* p. 89.
39. Adorno, T. W., et. al., *The Authoritarian Personality,* Harpers, New York, 1950. p. 150.
40. ——————, p. 849. * The conspiratorial mind-set also afflicts certain segments of the so-called left.
41. ——————, p. 856.
42. ——————, p. 872.
43. ——————, p. 976.
44. ——————, pp. 248-250.
45. Campbell, Donald T., and Thelma H. McCormack, "Military Experiences and Attitudes Toward Authority," *American Journal of Sociology,* LXII, March, 1957, pp. 482-290.
46. Janowitz, Morris, *Sociology and the Military Establishment,* Russell Sage Foundation, New York, 1959, p. 17.

47. Christie, R., "Changes in Authoritarianism as Related to Situational Factors," *American Psychologist*, VII, 1952, p. 307.
48. Hollander, E. D., *Leaders, Groups, and Influence*, Oxford Univ. Press, New York, 1964, p. 50.
49. This may be a significant factor in the problem the government has in getting men to join the Armed Forces without forceable conscription and in getting them to re-enlist when their time is up.
50. See E. D. Hollander, *op. cit.*, p. 46.
51. Janowitz, Morris, *op. cit.*, p. 18.
52. Mills, C. Wright, *The Power Elite*, Oxford Univ. Press, New York, 1959, pp. 186-187.
53. Bidwell, Charles E., "The Young Professional in the Army: A Study of Occupational Identity," *American Sociological Review*, XXVI, June 1961, p. 360.
54. Figures *exclude* veteran's benefits and services.
55. *Statistical Abstract of the United States*, 1966, 87th edition; 1968, 89th edition; and 1969, 90th edition.
56. Fred Cook says, "1,400 high-ranking officers have crossed the street and found retirement cushioned by lush salaries ladled out by the top 100 war contractors," *op. cit.*, p. 188.
57. Adapted from Albert D. Biderman, "Sequels to a Military Career: The Retired Military Professional," in *The New Military*, Russell Sage Foundation, edited by Morris Janowitz, pp. 298-299.
58. Art Buchwald spoofed this idea after a return to the Marines twenty years after his discharge. He found only three changes: 1) less physical punishment, 2) reciting prayers before eating, 3) a diet table for those overweight. *Life*, Aug. 13, 1965, pp. 71-81.
59. From the *Infantry Journal Reader*, 1943, p. 291.
60. Fourteen years later, in the official *Armed Forces Journal*, there is a slurring disregard to the facts of the Doolittle Inquiry in the statement: "With the exception of the occasional malcontent who was irreparably spoiled before he left home, American young men when brought into military organization do not resent rank," p. 28.
61. Spindler, G. Dearborn, "The Doolittle Board and Cooptation in the Army," *Social Forces*, 29:305-10 Mr. 51.
62. Janowitz, Morris, *op. cit.*, p. 38.
63. —————, p. 39.
64. —————, *The Professional Soldier*, The Glencoe Free Press, Glencoe, Illinois, 1960, pp. 405-406.
65. —————, p. 408.
66. —————, p. 410, Air Force quote from Department of the Air Force, AFR 55-11A, March 5, 1959, Air Force Psychological Operations, p. 26.

67. For a detailed study of this process see: Roger W. Little, "Buddy Relations and Combat Performance," in *The New Military,* pp. 195-223, *op. cit.*

68. Janowitz, Morris, *Sociology and the Military Establishment,* p. 79.

69. See Richard Christie, *An Experimental Study of Modification in Factors Influencing Recruits' Adjustment to the Army,* Research Center for Human Relations, New York University, 1953. Also, Hanan Charles Selvin, *The Effects of Leadership Climate on the Non-Duty Behavior*
(unpublished doctoral dissertation, Columbia University, 1956.)

70. Janowitz, Morris, *op. cit.,* p. 88.

71. President Kennedy's biographers have quoted him as saying, "The Navy has superhuman ability to screw up everything they touch . . . God save this country of ours from those patriots whose war cry is 'What this country needs is to be run with military efficiency'." From Theodore C. Sorenson, *Look,* Aug. 24, 1966, p. 40.

CHAPTER II

1. Huntington, Samuel, *The Soldier and the State,* The Belknap Press of Harvard Univ. Press, 1957, p. 79.

2. *Military Training* (FM 21-5), Dept. of the Army, Aug. 1959.

3. This same chapter is concluded with a list of basic conceptions of military training. The first one, stated with no indication of irony, is that "The dignity of the individual is not violated."

4. *Military Leadership* (FM 22-100), Dept. of the Army, June 1961.

5. —————, p. 9

6. —————, p. 14.

7. —————, p. 24.

8. —————, p. 36.

9. —————, p. 41.

10. —————, p. 42.

11. —————, p. 57.

12. —————, p. 60.

13. —————, p. 64.

14. *The Armed Forces Officer* (DOD Pam 1-20), 1961, p. 13.

15. —————, p. 27.

16. *The Armed Forces Officer, op. cit.,* p. 30.

17. —————, p. 100.

18. —————, p. 156.

19. For example, see *Military Guidance in Secondary Schools,* U.S. Government Printing Office, 1963, 0-692-489, pp. 20-21.

20. *The Armed Forces Officer,* op. cit., p. 160.

21. —————, p. 160.

22. —————, p. 171.

23. —————, p. 174.

24. ——————, p. 7.
25. ——————, p. 219.
26. ——————, p. 222.
27. ——————, p. 225.
28. ——————, p. 194.
29. ——————, p. 13.
30. ——————, p. 5.
31. *The Battle for Liberty,* Dept. of Defense Pamphlet 5-5, 1958, p. 21.
32. ——————, p. 140.
33. ——————, p. 143.
34. *Militant Liberty,* Office of Admiral Radford, 1955.
35. ——————, p. 5.
36. For example, see *The Battle for Liberty, op. cit.,* p. 23.
37. *Ideas in Conflict: Liberty and Communism,* Dept. of Defense Pamphlet 3-11, 1962.
38. See *Militant Liberty* and *Ideas in Conflict, op cit.*
39. *Battle for Liberty, op. cit.,* p. 23.
40. *The Fighting Man's Code, op. cit.,* pp. 6-7.
41. Torrance, E. Paul, *The Struggle for Men's Minds,* U.S.A.F., 1960.
42. By "The Fleet Leadership School, Fleet Training Center, U.S. Naval Station, San Diego, California."
43. In a discussion with the House Committee on Un-American Activities, Schwarz praised the Committee for its "magnificent educational job." He added, "You have certainly done a splendid educational job in revealing not only the theory, but the actual practice and character of Communism and Communists." See U.S. Government Printing Office document No. 92964.
44. *Alert,* No. 3, "The Truth About Our Economic System," Pam. 355-136, 1962; No. 5, "Soviet Treaty Violations," Pam. 355-138, 1962; No. 8, "We Will Bury You," AFP 190-1-10, 1963.

CHAPTER III

1. *New York Times,* July 22, 1957, Vol. 7, p. 5.
2. ——————, Vol. 7, p. 5.
3. Rockwell, George Lincoln, "Who Wants Panty-Waist Marines?," *American Mercury,* LXXXIV, April 1957, pp. 117-122.
4. ——————, Aug. 3, 1956, Vol. 1, p. 5.
5. *New York Times, op. cit.*
6. Burke, David, *Marine: The Life of Chesty Puller,* Little, Brown, & Co. (Bantam), 1962.
7. ——————, p. 2.
8. Kennedy, W. V., "Marine Corps Brutality," *America,* SCVIII, March 1, 1958.
9. Bigart, Homer, "Marines End Brutality in Drill," *New York Times,* April 12, 1959, Vol. 1, p. 4.

10. See *Life,* Oct. 10, 1969, p. 32.
11. *Honolulu Advertiser,* Nov. 8, 1969, p. A-4, column 8.
12. *Life,* Oct. 10, 1969, pp. 33-37.
13. Italics in these quotations are mine, to point out some of the more significant statements.
14. When one group of Marines left for Vietnam, the Marine commander gave a going away speech in which he said he ''Hoped they would find what they were looking for.'' One cannot be certain of what was intended but apparently the commander assumed that fulfillment was connected with killing the ''enemy,'' a grotesque modern version of the search for the Holy Grail.
15. This is prior to the time when Marines were sent to Vietnam.
16. Bettelheim, Bruno, *The Informed Heart,* Free Press, New York, 1962.
17. _____, p. 18.
18. _____, p. 271, (cf. sgt.-in-training film, ''You will do exactly. . . .'')
19. _____, p. 270.
20. _____, p. 294.
21. Fromm, Erich, *Escape from Freedom,* Farrar and Rinehart, New York, 1941.

CHAPTER IV

1. Power, Thomas S., *Design for Survival,* Coward-McCann, New York, 1964, p. 96.
2. _____, p. 85.
3. _____, p. 101.
4. _____, p. 44.
5. _____, p. 43.
6. _____, p. 126.
7. _____, p. 231.
8. See Richard J. Barnet, *Intervention and Revolution,* World Publishing Co., 1968.
9. _____, p. 258.
10. See Jerome B. Wiesner and Herbert F. York, ''National Security and the Nuclear Test Ban,'' *Scientific American,* Oct. 1964.
11. Brown, Harrison and James Real, *Community of Fear,* Center for the Study of Democratic Institutions, 1960, pp. 14-17.
12. See Ruth Benedict, *Patterns of Culture,* Houghton-Mifflin, New York, 1934.
13. Berman, Harold J., ''The Devil and Soviet Russia,'' *The American Scholar,* XXVII, Spring, 1958, p. 149.
14. Melman, Seymour, *Our Depleted Society,* Holt-Rinehart, and Winston, New York, 1965, p. 4.
15. Friedman, Saul, ''The RAND Corporation and Our Policy Makers,'' *The Atlantic Monthly,* CCXII, Sept. 1963, p. 68.

16. Mills, C. Wright, *Causes of World War III*, Simon and Schuster, New York, p. 47.
17. See Raoul Naroll, "Does Military Deterrence Deter?," *Transaction*, Jan.-Feb. 1966, pp. 14-20.
18. Cited in Henry Steele Commager, "A Historian Looks at Our Political Morality," *Saturday Review*, July 10, 1965, p. 16.
19. Cited in Tristram Coffin, *The Armed Society*, Pelican Books, 1964, p. 48.
20. When Lyndon Johnson was in the House of Representatives in 1948, he stated that without superior air power we would be easy "prey to any yellow dwarf with a pocket knife." See *Congressional Record*, XCIV, part II, p. 2883.
21. Toynbee, Arnold, "Supersam," *Ramparts*, Dec. 1965, p. 44.
22. Sears, Louis M., *A History of American Foreign Relations*, Crowell, New York, 1927, pp. 414-421.
23. —————— , pp. 462-466.
24. Commager, *op. cit.*, pp. 17-18.
25. See Fred Cook, "The CIA," *The Nation*, June 24, 1961. Also Fred Cook, "CIA: The Case Builds Up," *The Nation*, June 22, 1964, pp. 616-618.
26. Greene, Felix, "Peking Said Anticipating U.S. Attack," A.P. report in the Honolulu Star Bulletin, Dec. 27, 1965, pp. 5-6.
27. See Arthur Larson, *Questions and Answers on the World Court*, World Rule of Law Center, Duke University, 1964, pp. 30-44.
28. Beale, Howard, *Are American Teachers Free?*, Charles Scribner's Sons, 1936, New York, p. 19.
29. Cousins, Norman, "Back to the Fundamentals," *Saturday Review*, Nov. 6, 1965, p. 26.
30. Fixx, James F., "A Startled Look at British Television," *Saturday Review*, Nov. 13, 1965, pp. 98-100.
31. This is explained in the latter section of this chapter, "The American Contribution to the Cold War."
32. Coffin, Tristam, *The Armed Society*, Penguin Books, p. 12
33. *The History of Violence in America*. A report on the causes and prevention of violence; Bantam, 1969. Quoted from an introduction by John Herbers.
34. ——————————————————— ,
    pp. 63-64.
35. McClintock, Inez and Marshall, *Toys in America*, Public Affairs Press, Washington, D. C., 1961.
36. Lehman, H. and P. Witty, *The Psychology of Play Activities*, A. S. Barnes and Co., New York, 1927.
37. See William H. Honan, "Merry Bang-Bang and Happy New Year," *The New Republic*, Dec. 25, 1965, pp.11-12.
38. Berkowitz, Leonard and Eda Rawlings, "Effects of Film Violence on

Inhibitions Against Subsequent Aggression,'' *Journal of Abnormal and Social Psychology,* LXVI, No. 5, 1963, pp. 405-412.

39. Marmor, Judd, ''War Violence and Human Nature,'' *Bulletin of the Atomic Scientists,* March 1964.

40. Quoted in the *National Peace Education Bulletin* of ''Women Strike for Peace,'' II, Dec. 1965, p. 2.

41. This is *in addition* to possible compulsory high school and college ROTC.

42. Ministers of religion have, strangely enough, been exempted. Possibly this helps silence some of them against the moral issues of conscription and the war.

43. John Galbraith points out that ''The Great Depression of the thirties never came to an end. It merely disappeared in the great mobilization of the forties,'' in *American Capitalism,* Harmondsworth, 1963, p. 78.

44. Truman, Harry S., *Memoirs,* Doubleday, New York, 1955, Vol. I, p. 511.

45. An AP report in the *Honolulu Star-Bulletin,* Oct. 21, 1965, p. A-7.

46. See Kenneth Keniston, *The Young Radicals,* Harcourt, Brace, & Co., 1968.

47. In the *Annals of the American Academy of Political and Social Science,* Jan. 1966., p. 132.

48. Early in 1966, David Mitchell of Brooklyn faced a court trial based on refusal to report for induction. He claimed that he could not avoid violating either the draft law or the international law of the Nuremberg trials, since they contradict each other. At the time he was to be drafted, he might be sent to Vietnam in a war which Mitchell says involves ''crimes against humanity.'' Mitchell lost his first case, received a sentence of five years imprisonment, appealed, but the Supreme Court refused to review his appeal.

49. See George F. Kennan, *Russian Leaves the War,* Princeton University Press, Princeton, New Jersey, 1956.

50. Neal, Fred, *U.S. Foreign Policy and the Soviet Union,* Center for the Study of Democratic Institutions, 1961, p. 9. This is an excellent account of the basis for American-Soviet conflicts, showing that there have not been good guys and bad guys, but only some people doing a good deal of harm to each other, largely through misunderstanding.

51. Alperovitz, Gar, *Atomic Diplomacy,* Simon and Schuster, New York, 1965, p. 13.

52. _____, p. 155.

53. _____, pp. 236-237.

54. _____, p. 227.

55. _____, p. 226.

56. _____, p. 226

57. _____, p. 235.

58. _____, p. 235.

59. —————————, p. 124.
60. —————————, p. 27.
61. —————————, p. 235.
62. —————————, p. 58.
63. —————————, p. 58.
64. —————————, p. 200.
65. —————————, p. 200.
66. Ismay, H., *The Memoirs of Lord Ismay,* Heinemann, London, 1960, p. 401.
67. Millis, Walter, *Individual Freedom and the Common Defense,* The Fund for the Republic, Nov. 1957.
68. In *The Free World Colossus,* Hill and Wang, 1965. Also see P. M. S. Blackett, *Fear, War, and the Bomb,* Whittlesey House. In 1948, Blackett stated that ''the dropping of the atomic bomb was not so much the last military act of the Second World War, as the first major operation of the cold war with Russia.'' Also, see Fred Neal, ''Government by Myth'' *The Center Magazine,* Nov. 1969, pp. 2-7.
69. Kennan, George, *Russia, the Atom, and the West,* Harper, New York, 1958, p. 41.
70. Warburg, James P., *The West in Crisis,* Doubleday, New York, 1959, p. 157.
71. Taylor, Harold, ''How Credible Are Our Professions of Peace?,'' *The Progressive,* March 1963.
72. Possibly this was a countervailing political policy to ''make-up'' for the progressive reforms he asked for in domestic policy.
73. Cousins, Norman, *Saturday Review,* March 5, 1966, p. 30.
74. Melman, Seymour, *Our Depleted Society,* Holt-Rinehart & Winston, 1965.
75. —————————, p. 4.
76. See Harold D. Lasswell, ''The Garrison-State Hypothesis Today?'' in Changing Patterns of Military Politics, Glencoe Free Press, Glencoe, Illinois, edited by Samuel P. Huntington, 1964, pp. 51-70.
77. —————————, p. 145.
78. Fulbright, J. William, *Old Myths and New Realities,* Random House, New York, 1964, pp. 3-4.
79. See Arnold Toynbee, ''Supersam,'' *Ramparts,* Dec. 1965, p. 47.
80. Neal, Fred, ''U.S. Foreign Policy and the Soviet Union,'' *Center for the Study of Democratic Institution,* 1961, pp. 53-54.
81. For instance, see Robert Scheer, *How the United States Got Involved in Vietnam,* Center for the Study of Democratic Institutions, 1965.
82. See Norman Cousins, ''Vietnam: The Spurned Peace,'' *Saturday Review,* July 26, 1969. Secretary Rusk avoided an opportunity to negotiate with the North Vietnamese. Instead, he supported the bombing of North Vietnam with the explanation that the bombing was designed to get North Vietnam to negotiate. Such action suggests that

he really wanted to subjugate North Vietnam through American military power rather than to negotiate.

83. See Mark A. May, ''War is Not a Human Instinct,'' in *A Social Psychology of War and Peace,* Yale University, 1943, Chapter 2.

84. See Ruth Benedict, *Patterns of Culture,* Mentor, New York, 1948.

85. Not in all Americans, to be sure, but in those who guide the central course of American policy.

86. Fromm, Erich, *May Man Prevail?,* Anchor, New York, 1961, pp. 17-30.

87. Shoup, Gen. David M., ''The New American Militarism,'' *The Atlantic,* 1969, pp. 51-56.

CHAPTER V

1. See Michael Harrington, *The Accidental Century,* Macmillan, New York, 1965.

2. See William Boyer, ''Have Our Schools Kept Us Free,'' *School Review,* Summer 1963.

3. See Annette Zelman, *Teaching About Communism in American Schools,* Humanities Press, New Yok, 1965, pp. 5-8.

4. This includes a whole range of programs for both boys and girls from ages 7 or 8 to adulthood.

5. A recent radio spot for the Boy Scouts criticized protestors and indicated that scout training would prevent this from happening to ''your boy.''

6. ''Citizenship-Month Activities,'' *Montana Education,* April 1967, pp. 26-28.

7. See Gladys Wiggins, *Education and Nationalism,* McGraw-Hill, 1962, pp. 4-6.

8. ''Military Training: A Critical Appraisal,'' *Progressive Education,* 1935, p. 8.

9. ''Main Issues in the Junior ROTC Controversy,'' *Harvard Education Review,* IX, Oct. 1939, p. 480.

10. Same title, in *The Nation's Schools,* IV, Sept. 1929, pp. 27-29.

11. Rogers, Herbert W., ''Some Attitudes of Students in the ROTC,'' *Journal of Educational Psychology,* XXVI, 1935, pp. 291-306.

12. Droste, Edward P. and Warren C. Seyfert, ''Attitudes and Activities of Graduates of a Military School,'' *School Review,* Oct. 1941, pp. 587-594.

13. Seates, Douglas E. and Dale K. Spenser, ''Retroactive Experiment on Effects on Military Training in High School,'' *School Review,* March 1941, pp. 195-204.

14. Nelson, Gaylord A., ''Personality and Attitude Differences Associated with the Elective Substitution of ROTC for Physical Education Requirement in High School,'' *Research Quarterly: Personality and Attitude Differences,* March 1948, Vol. 19, pp. 2-17.

15. Information is taken from the *Junior ROTC Manual,* Dept. of the Army, ROTCM 145-4-1, June 1962; also from *The Congressional Record,* Sept. 28, 1964, pp. 22262-22268.
16. See ROTC Units and NDCC Units, Dept. of the Army, AGPB-P, Feb. 1963; also *Congressional Record,* Sept. 28, 1964, p. 22262.
17. Paul, Norman, Assistant Secretary of Defense, *Congressional Record,* Sept. 28, 1964, p. 22265.
18. _____, p. 22265.
19. *Congressional Record,* CX, No. 186, p. 22267.
20. _____, p. 22267.
21. Cook, Fred, *The Warfare State,* Macmillan, 1962, p. 181.
22. "ROTC Revitalization," *op. cit.*
23. _____, p. 56.
24. _____, p. 58.
25. _____, p. 67.
26. In a letter to Professor Robert Potter of the University of Hawaii, Senator Inouye said, "There are many thousands of young men in Hawaii, such as I, who have undergone this training and have not turned out to be militarists in any sense of that word." A year later, the Senator was one of the major congressional supporters of Junior ROTC, and he was a strong supporter of President Johnson's policy in Vietnam. Only after the Republican take-over of the administration in 1969 did Inouye begin to openly criticize the war.
27. "ROTC Revitalization," *op. cit.,* p. 68.
28. _____, p. 69.
29. The notable exceptions were Senators Gaylord Nelson and Representative Robert Kastenmeier, who offered excellent counter-arguments but apparently lacked the "divisions."
30. See Merle Curti, *The Social Ideas of American Educators,* Charles Scribner's Sons, New York, 1935, p. 589.
31. Torrance, Paul E., *The Struggle for Men's Minds,* USAF, Washington, D. C., 1960, p. 98.
32. _____, p. 98.
33. _____, p. 98.
34. See G. M. Lyons and J. W. Masland, *Education and Military Leadership,* Princeton University Press, Princeton, New Jersey, 1959, p. 30.
35. _____, p. 44.
36. Cited in V. T. Thayer, *Formative Ideas in American Education,* Dodd, Mead, and Co., New York, 1965, p. 277.
37. Lyons, G. M., *op. cit.,* p. 45.
38. _____, p. 47.
39. _____, p. 47.
40. _____, p. 168.

41. Brick, Allan, *American Association of University Professors' Bulletin,* XLV, June 1959, pp. 218-222.

42. _____, pp. 218-222.

43. _____, p. 173.

44. _____, p. 175.

45. It should be pointed out that some of the regular college and university staff have essentially the same outlook as ROTC instructors, and their failure to have students examine issues also makes them quite interchangeable with a totalitarian system of higher education.

46. In the 1962 *West Point Catalogue.*

47. Boroff, David, *Harpers,* 1962, Vol. 225, No. 1351, p. 59.

48. From the 1968-69 *West Point Catalogue.*

49. ROTCM 145-20.

50. _____, p. 72.

51. _____, p. 80.

52. ROTCM, p. 228.

53. _____, p. 228.

54. _____145-101, Sept. 1969, p. 19.

55. _____, p. 27.

56. _____, p. 172.

57. "ROTC Vitalization Act of 1964." Hearing before the Committee on Armed Service, U. S. Senate, 88th Congress on H. R. 9124, Aug. 13, 1964, p. 58.

58. Lyons, G. M., *op. cit,* p. 219.

59. *The College Student and the ROTC,* George Washington University Bureau of Social Science Research Inc., Washington, D. C., Sept. 1958.

60. See Joseph W. Scott, "ROTC Retreat," *Transaction,* Sept. 1969, pp. 47-52.

61. Ridgeway, James, *The Closed Corporation: American Universities in Crisis,* Ballantine Books, 1968, p. 113.

62. _____, p. 136.

63. Commager, Henry Steele, "The University as Employment Agency," *New Republic,* Feb. 24, 1968.

64. See "Professors of the Silent Generation," Lyle A. Downing and Jerome J. Salome, *Transaction,* June 1969, p. 43-45.

65. Rosak, Theodore, *The Dissenting Academy,* Vintage, 1967, p. 12.

CHAPTER VI

1. See Kenneth Boulding, "The Prevention of World War III," p. 5, and Herman Kahn "The Arms Race and Some of its Hazards," p. 21, in *Toward a Theory of War Prevention,* edited by Richard Falk and Saul Mendlovitz, World Law Fund, 1967.

2. Clark, Grenville and Louis B. Sohn, *World Peace through World Law,* Harvard University Press, 1966, 3rd ed., 535 pp.

3. See Charles Osgood's *An Alterative to War or Surrender.*
4. Falk, Richard, "Songmy: War Crimes and Individual Respon-sibility," *Transaction,* Jan. 1970, pp. 33-40.
5. See Archibald S. Alexander, "The Cost of World Armaments," *Scientific American,* Oct. 1969, pp. 21-27.
6. See Ian L. McHarg, "Man and Environment" in *The Urban Con-dition,* ed. by Leonard J. Duhl, Basic Books, 1963.
7. Henry, Jules, "The G.I. Syndrome," *Transaction,* I, May 1964, p.9.
8. To say nothing of numerous other government aids to the rich from airline and farm subsidies to oil depletion allowances.
9. Members of the Committee: Kenneth Binder, (William Boyer), Francis Brennen, Judith Casey, Prof. Willis Griffin, James Houston, Ronald Miyamura, William Redding, Glenn Sakai, Mary Teves, Karen Tsukamoto.

Materials and bibliographies on anti-war education can be obtained by writing to the following organizations:

1. WORLD LAW FUND
   11 West 42nd Street, New York, New York 10036
2. WORLD WITHOUT WAR COUNCIL (Regional Offices)
   National: 218 E. 18th St., New York, N. Y. 10003
   Midwest: 116 S. Michigan, Chicago, Illinois 60603
   Northwest: 4235 Roosevelt Way, N.E., Seattle, Washington 98105
   Pacific Central: 1730 Grove, Berkeley, California 94709
   New England: 144-A Mt. Auburn St., Cambridge, Mass. 02138
3. CENTER FOR THE STUDY OF DEMOCRATIC INSTITUTIONS
   Box 4068, Santa Barbara, California
4. AMERICAN FRIENDS SERVICE COMMITTEE
   160 North Fifteenth Street, Philadelphia, Pennsylvania 19102

The following journals provide continuous access to current ideas and research:

1. WAR/PEACE REPORT
   218 East 18th Street
   New York, N.Y. 10003

   (General and readable. Appropriate for use by high school students, college students, and teachers.)

2. BULLETIN OF THE ATOMIC SCIENTISTS
   935 E. 60th Street
   Chicago, Illinois 60637

   (Includes general and specialized material. An indispensible source for teachers of science and social studies.)

3. JOURNAL OF CONFLICT RESOLUTION
   University of Michigan
   Ann Arbor, Michigan 48104

   (A technical journal of social science research bearing on issues of war and peace.)